SACRAMENTO PUBLIC LIBRARY
828 "I" STREET
SACRAMENTO, CA 95814
3/2013

Gonzo Judaism

Also by Niles Elliot Goldstein

The Challenge of the Soul:
A Guide for the Spiritual Warrior

Craving the Divine:
A Spiritual Guide for Today's Perplexed

Lost Souls:
Finding Hope in the Heart of Darkness

God at the Edge:
Searching for the Divine in Uncomfortable
and Unexpected Places

Spiritual Manifestos:
Visions for Renewed Religious Life in
America from Young Spiritual Leaders
of Many Faiths (editor)

Duties of the Soul:
The Role of Commandments in Liberal Judaism
(edited with Peter S. Knobel)

Forests of the Night:
The Fear of God in Early Hasidic Thought

Judaism and Spiritual Ethics
(with Steven S. Mason)

Gonzo
JUDAISM

A Bold Path for
Renewing an
Ancient Faith

RABBI NILES ELLIOT
GOLDSTEIN

 TRUMPETER Boston & London 2010

Trumpeter Books
An imprint of Shambhala Publications, Inc.
Horticultural Hall
300 Massachusetts Avenue
Boston, Massachusetts 02115
www.shambhala.com

© 2006 by Niles Elliot Goldstein

All rights reserved. No part of this book may be
reproduced in any form or by any means, electronic
or mechanical, including photocopying, recording, or by
any information storage and retrieval system, without
permission in writing from the publisher.

9 8 7 6 5 4 3 2 1

First Paperback Edition

Printed in Canada

⊗ This edition is printed on acid-free paper that meets
the American National Standards Institute Z39.48 Standard.
♻ This book was printed on 100% postconsumer recycled paper.
For more information please visit www.shambhala.com.
Distributed in the United States by Random House, Inc.,
and in Canada by Random House of Canada Ltd

Library of Congress Cataloging-in-Publication Data
Goldstein, Niles Elliot, 1966–
  Gonzo Judaism: a bold path for renewing an ancient faith /
Niles Elliot Goldstein. — [1st paperback ed.]
  p. cm.
Reprint. Originally published: New York: St. Martin's Press, 2006.
ISBN 978-1-59030-768-7 (pbk.: alk. paper)
1. Spiritual life—Judaism. 2. Jewish way of life.
3. Judaism—Customs and practices. I. Title.
BM723.G66 2010
296.7—dc22
2009026466

For Michele

CONTENTS

INTRODUCTION

ONE OF THE SURE SIGNS you've entered the world of gonzo is that you often find yourself feeling uneasy and agitated—not angry, really, so much as indignant toward the inane behavior and sheer idiocy of the powers that be. Another is that you feel a deep cynicism and a biting urge to *revolt,* directly and personally, against the establishment causing your discomfort. You want to get off your ass and jump into the fray. You want to do battle with the Machine, whatever and wherever the Machine might be.

Hunter S. Thompson was the guru of the gonzo form of journalism in the sixties and seventies. What he fought was the dispassionate, "objective" approach to news writing that was so prevalent in his field at the time. Thompson's approach to the stories he covered was intensely personal and opinionated—he embedded himself in everything he wrote about, from the violent Hell's Angels motorcycle gang to the seedy culture of Las Vegas. He was outrageous and, not infrequently, offensive. Like the blast of a ram's horn on Rosh Hashanah, Thompson's words shook people up, kept them awake, and forced them to think and see in new ways.

That's what a gonzo form of Judaism can do in our own era.

I first felt the gonzo impulse for myself a few years ago,

when the Southern Baptist Convention came out with a public statement in which they said that as part of their continuing mission to spread the "good news" and try to win converts to Christianity, they would start to proselytize actively among members of the Jewish community. I was a freshly minted rabbi and, at the time, still read all the Jewish papers and magazines. The reaction from the Jewish leadership was swift, uniform, and unequivocal. Full-page denunciations were published in major newspapers across the country. Familiar talking heads appeared on *Nightline* and throughout the national media, saying: *Anti-Semitic assault! Bible-thumpers coming after our sons and daughters! A new Holocaust!*

I was furious. Yet my outrage seemed to stand in stark disconnect from that of most other rabbis and executives of Jewish organizations, who demanded that other Baptist and Christian leaders denounce the plan. While I found, and find, the evangelical focus on proselytization to be highly problematic, even ungodly, these Baptists were just being true to their fundamentalist theology. I wasn't mad at them—I was angry with us. Our real adversary wasn't this Southern Baptist denomination, but ourselves. If we'd only offer American Jews—especially younger and searching ones—a Judaism that was vibrant, inspiring, edgy, and joyful, rather than one that was fearful, defensive, ossified, and out of touch with the needs and desires of a new generation of Jews, no one would even be *tempted* to look elsewhere for their spiritual sustenance.

I wanted to say to both these Baptists and my colleagues: "Go ahead, come at me with your best shot. I'm standing my ground, and I'm standing it confidently and proudly. I'm not going anywhere."

I felt the gonzo impulse again, even more intensely, with the release of Mel Gibson's controversial movie *The Passion of the Christ*. Though several years had passed since their open warfare with these Southern Baptists, the reaction of Jewish leaders was nearly identical. Angry protestations appeared in the papers and filled the airwaves and television screens. The usual suspects—the same individuals who'd spoken out against these Baptists—were interviewed by the press over and over again. What did they have to say about the film? *Anti-Semitic! Dangerous! A recipe for modern pogroms!*

Holy crap, I thought. What a waste of energy, time, and resources—all of which could (and should) have been put to better use creating the kind of Judaism our people so passionately crave. I offered some of these opinions to the press myself, but I was in the vast, almost silent (or ignored) minority. Then, in our celebrity-driven culture, there was the other burning question: Was Mel Gibson himself an anti-Semite? I didn't know and I didn't care. While his film, as most serious scholars noted, was a clear distortion of very murky historical events described in the Gospels, it was *his* film, and he had a right to make it. All our leaders ultimately did was give the movie the kind of publicity that studios only dream about. *The Passion* became an enormous Hollywood blockbuster, not in spite of the Jewish community, but in part because of it.

Even now, as time has passed and emotions have cooled, I have no idea as to whether or not Mel Gibson is truly anti-Semitic. I *do* think that, at a minimum, he's shown himself to be an insensitive, arrogant schmuck and a bit of a moron for not having treated the complexities of the Gospels with more care and attention to nuance—but we were pretty moronic ourselves in our handling of the situation. For me, the troubling bottom line is that whatever their intentions were, Jewish communal leaders turned out to be, once more, our community's own worst enemies.

As a rabbi and as an American Jew, of this I am certain: We

don't want or need more of the same. I'm sick of watching the same hangdog, lachrymose faces of older men—and they're invariably older and male—uttering their same reactionary, predictable, alarmist messages about what great, grave danger the Jewish people are in. I'm sick of Abe Foxman (of the Anti-Defamation League), sick of Rabbi Marvin Heir (of the Simon Wiesenthal Center), even sick of Elie Wiesel.

Tough words? You bet. But somebody, especially a person in a position of Jewish authority, needs to say them. I'm sick and tired of being sick and tired.

What we need for this next generation and century—and what we need desperately—are new faces and new voices. The messages must be different as well, in content and in spirit. Not the familiar messages rooted in insecurity and fear, but fresh ones grounded in confidence and celebration. Who in their right mind would want to be part of a religious community whose motto, based on its past behavior, might as well be "Come Survive with Us"? I, for one, don't want to merely survive—I want to thrive. Let's get the hell over our fears and anxieties about anti-Semitism, assimilation, and intermarriage. Let's get out from under the shadow of the Holocaust. Let's build an American Judaism—both in and out of the synagogue—that is joyous, vigorous, vivacious, even audacious.

I refuse to look cautiously over my shoulder; I'm staring straight ahead. And what I see is possibility. Wonderful possibility.

For many years the mantra of the Jewish establishment has been "Continuity, Continuity, Continuity." But Jewish history itself proves that it has been *dis*continuity that has often led to the most profound, imaginative, successful, and long-lasting outcomes for our faith and our community. I would argue that it's been the gonzo impulse—the urge to rupture, rebel, revolt, take risks—that has served as the dynamic life force of Judaism.

The prophets themselves, from Isaiah to Hosea and beyond, all cried out—often with passion and fury—for radical changes in the biblical societies to which they belonged. Sometimes at great personal risk, they called truth to power. They advocated self-examination. They uncovered the nakedness of kings and shook the status quo to its very core. They shouted heroically and alone from the margins of their world, from the edges of their communities.

Though a lot of contemporary Jewish leaders are worried about our future as a religious community, our own past seems to say that we'll be just fine. It's not about numbers, and it never has been. In recent years the heads of some of the Jewish movements debated in the press about which of them could claim more affiliated members. Who gives a damn? Two thousand years ago, in the tiny village of Yavneh, a small group of Palestinian rabbis boldly transformed the Temple-based religion they had inherited. In the sixteenth century an even smaller number of Kabbalists in the Galilee (most of them in their twenties and thirties) reshaped the Sabbath liturgy into the form that is familiar to us now, whether we live in Fargo or Fez.

Size doesn't matter. What matters is commitment and creativity.

We need that same commitment today, that same audacity and willingness to think—and act—outside the box. We need to reach the disaffected, namely, most of us, in order to construct new models and approaches to Jewish life. Urging people to become more active Jews through the use of guilt; sending out alarming fundraising letters that imply there's a knife-toting skinhead hovering at the corner; building Holocaust memorials in nearly every major city around the country—none of these things are going to make largely disinterested Jews want to embrace or pass on their Jewish identities and spiritual traditions. What we must create instead is a Jewish culture and community rooted in affirmation, joy, and celebration, not guilt, fear, and sentimentality.

The fiddler on the roof can take his fiddle and stick it where the sun don't shine.

And so the gonzo spirit must live on, the same spirit that motivated the prophets to lambast their unjust societies and the mystics to daringly compose new prayers that have lasted for centuries. But now it's our turn. We must be willing to enter the fray and fight. We must climb down from those Himalayan peaks, from the escapism of more "exotic" Eastern religions, and come home. Judaism will only change if we follow the lead of our forebears and change it ourselves. Are we up to this challenge? Are we willing to break from the herd and run with an alternative, unconventional, and sometimes brazen crowd? Are we brave enough to take risks, including the risk of failure?

Who knows what a truly revitalized and remodeled Judaism will look like—we may not know for decades or more, long after we're dead and buried. But one thing is certain: This is a historic, transitional moment in Jewish life, and our generation is living in it. We can act as spectators and let it pass us by.

Or we can leap into the muck and mire of our imaginations, as well as into our rich and profound religious heritage, and take a ride with the angels.

Let the old people wallow in the shame of having failed. The laws they made to preserve a myth are no longer pertinent; the so-called American Way begins to seem like a dike made of cheap cement, with many more leaks than the law has fingers to plug. America has been breeding mass anomie since the end of World War II. It is not a political thing, but the sense of new realities, of urgency, anger, and sometimes desperation in a society where even the highest authorities seem to be grasping at straws.

—HUNTER S. THOMPSON, *Hell's Angels*

Behold! I have put my words into your mouth. Bear witness! I have made you an overseer this day over nations and kingdoms— to uproot and to tear down, to destroy and to overthrow, to build and to plant.

—JEREMIAH 1:9–10

Gonzo Judaism

CHAPTER 1

Get Out of Your Damn Head— and into Your Gut

I T WAS DEFINITELY OLD SCHOOL. You had the tall, stained-glass windows, the vast and vaulted ceiling, long rows of fixed pews, the professional choir singing from behind a screen, the omnipresent organ, and the clergy wearing black polyester robes.

The worship service was very high church—but this place was a synagogue.

I had been invited to give a guest lecture at a large, affluent congregation in a New York suburban area. During the Sabbath service and prior to my remarks, I'd been sitting on an elevated stagelike structure, a *bimah,* in one of the seats reserved for clergy and other "special people," like synagogue presidents and local politicians.

You don't like to bite the hand that feeds you, so I sat politely and patiently through all of the liturgical "Thees" and "Thous," the operatic, nonparticipatory music, the formal and rigid choreography of sitting and standing at the appropriate moments, and the English responsive readings performed in perfect unison.

I felt like a caged animal.

Still, I was a young rabbi with a job to do, and I was grateful for the opportunity to expose this staid, conservative community to a little Jewish mysticism. I had recently returned from a summer adventure in Central Asia, through the newly independent nations of Kazakhstan, Kyrgyzstan, and Uzbekistan. The Judaism that I was exposed to there—raw, tribal, and impassioned—had opened my eyes to a more visceral form of Jewish life than I had known here in the United States.

As I sat before the congregation, I was wearing a token of my trip through the Silk Road—an oversized, brightly colored yarmulke that was customarily worn by men in that remote, ancient region, both at services and on the street. With the exception of four or five other congregants, everyone else was bareheaded. But I didn't think much about my yarmulke. I just liked the way it looked, as well as the way it felt as it embraced my skull.

Toward the end of the service I gave my talk, in which I examined some of the core teachings and myths of Lurianic Kabbalah, a bold (and somewhat subversive) sixteenth-century twist on classical Jewish mysticism. I presented its radical ideas about creation and redemption and explained its focus on intuition rather than reason as the key to unlocking the mysteries of the universe as well as those of the soul. I discussed how, for Rabbi Isaac Luria and his circle of disciples, human beings were viewed—literally—as miniature worlds, as conveyed through the Kabbalistic aphorism *Adam hu olam katan* (Man is a microcosmos). What this meant was that the boundary between the finite and the Infinite was far more porous than most of us have been led to believe by mainstream Judaism.

When I finished I invited the congregation to ask me any

questions they might have. The senior rabbi walked up to the lectern and whispered, "We don't do that here."

After the service I spent a few minutes with the senior rabbi in his lavish office, with its dark wood paneling, huge desk and high chair, bay windows, and walls dotted with photographs of the rabbi shaking hands with a few former vice presidents and foreign ministers. Save for the religious texts on one of the walls, I could just as easily have been in the office of the CEO of Merrill Lynch or Smith Barney.

"Quite an interesting talk," said the senior rabbi, an impeccably groomed man in his sixties who is a respected figure in the Jewish establishment. But his intonation of the word "interesting" made it sound like what he really meant was, "Not bad for an upstart punk, but you've got a lot to learn about being a rabbi in today's world."

I thanked him for the opportunity to speak from his pulpit and I wished him well.

"There's just one thing," he added.

"Oh?" I asked.

"The yarmulke."

A dramatic pause. I instinctively—almost protectively— reached for the top of my head. "This? What about it?"

"It's just—it's just not in the spirit of the Sabbath. Its striking size, all those vivid colors . . . The Sabbath is about sober reflection and contemplation. That yarmulke is not dignified or decorous. It's primitive. It conveys too much emotion."

Is this guy for real? I wondered. Not in the spirit of the Sabbath? Too much emotion? What does this overripe, trapped-in-his-brain cleric think a Sabbath ceremony should feel like—a funeral?

I remember musing to myself, *I'll be sure to stay very sober and calm the next time. You're absolutely right—this yarmulke represents a dangerous and slippery slope. The harder stuff is right*

around the corner. Before you know it, I'll be drinking rat poison,
playing with snakes, and speaking in tongues.

Though this episode occurred several years ago, it is emblematic
of one of the great pathologies of modern Jewry and of Westerners in general—our inability to get out of our heads, and our
incapacity to trust our hearts. This is partly the residue of the
Enlightenment, a complex historical event that opened humanity's eyes and minds, but in some ways closed its soul.
While its emphasis on reason and scientific method led to
great advances in industry, technology, social structure, medicine, and our knowledge about ourselves and the universe, its
inherent triumphalism—and dogmatism—dismissed most
forms of faith as mere superstition, and gradually reshaped organized religion in its own image.

Religious institutions were gutted of any deep emotionality
and instead became seats of cerebralism: Liturgies became
statements of creed rather than expressions of yearning; ser-
mons became rarefied and highly intellectual, often referring
to God in a distanced, detached way, as "the Deity" rather than
by one of the many personal names found in the Bible; the
clergy, dressed in academic-looking gowns, led services and
preached from lofty platforms far removed from their congregants below; and religious rituals, unless they were compatible
with rational explanation, took a backseat to words or disappeared entirely.

In defiance of this phenomenon, there were voices of
protest. Nietzsche, though not religious in a formal sense, declared that he lived in the age of the death of God—and he
didn't declare it with glee. Kierkegaard, who argued that faith
was an act of the will, not of the mind, castigated his bourgeois
Copenhagen community for killing off Christianity. And even
in the less cosmopolitan, more rural environment of Eastern

European Jewry, a brash and populist mystical movement—Hasidism—emerged, largely in opposition to the overly rationalistic and legalistic Judaism of the time. Hasidism claimed that the lifeblood of Judaism was its spirituality, its genius for uncovering sanctity and mystery in seemingly commonplace activities like eating, drinking, and sex. Making love on the Sabbath, for instance, was viewed as one of the highest levels of spiritual expression.

Enlightenment ideas formed the bedrock of our own society and bestowed authority to the powers that ran it, and though changes are certainly afoot today, for most of us the head still trumps the heart. That's why my colorful, distinctly *un*sober yarmulke bothered that rabbi so much. He saw it, probably unconsciously, as a threat—to his worldview, to his take on religion, even to his ecclesiastical position. Why else would an intelligent, well-educated man make as stupid a statement as he did?

The Jewish Sabbath—Shabbat—isn't simply about "sober reflection and contemplation." Shabbat is about many things, including quiet rumination, but fundamentally it is about the affirmation and celebration of life itself. It is our coat of many colors, the beautiful garment Jews get to wrap ourselves in every seventh day. Shabbat is the quintessence of *oneg,* of joyfulness.

So is Judaism.

When we lose sight of that fact, when we take the joy out of Judaism, we begin to destroy the very thing we supposedly love.

In the movie *Jerry Maguire* Tom Cruise plays a sports agent whose client wants Cruise's character to demonstrate, not just talk about, his allegiance and commitment to the player's football career and family. With the famous phrase "Show me the money!" the wide receiver tosses out a challenge and a charge.

He is asking his agent to do his job—but he is also asking him to prove his love.

How deeply passionate are our religious leaders, our agents of Jewish life and practice? If we really, truly loved our Judaism, wouldn't we want to share it with—and demonstrate it to—others in an emotional, heartfelt way? Maybe we rabbis need a good kick in the butt from the Jewish community in order to get our blood flowing, to *feel* rather than just talk. Maybe we need you to shout, "Show me the passion!"

Jews have been voting with their feet, and those feet have been walking in places other than the aisles of synagogues. The majority of contemporary Jews do not belong to congregations. According to the 2000–2001 National Jewish Population Survey, only 46 percent of the 5.2 million Jews in America belong to congregations. That percentage is by all accounts dramatically lower for those under the age of thirty-five, a crucial demographic that the NJPS didn't even bother to poll. Modern Judaism, so heavily influenced by the ideas of the Enlightenment, is not speaking to people. Yet that's not just the fault of the synagogue; it's also the fault of Jews ourselves for not getting over our baggage from the lousy Hebrew school experiences we had as children, or, perhaps on a subconscious level, for not being able to relinquish some of our own reliance on reason and to begin to trust our hearts and our guts to lead us down the right path.

We've created a catch-22 situation—we don't practice Judaism because it seems too intellectualized and doesn't touch our souls, yet we're afraid of genuinely letting go, of exposing ourselves, of the uncertainties of faith.

There are some Jewish groups out there willing to take risks, to experiment with more emotional modes of Jewish expression and identity. That's a start. But, sadly, all too often these groups fall into the trap of *anti*-intellectualism, opening up one of our God-given capacities while shutting off the other. We see this in certain sectors of the Jewish Renewal movement, in its communities and teachers. Their warm and fuzzy brand of Judaism may wash down easily, and it may focus more on emotionality, but like any kind of comfort food it will ultimately make us sleepy and lethargic. My personal experiences in Renewal communities have usually felt like therapy sessions—a lot of talking, a lot of self-expression, a lot of outpouring of feelings.

My brain, however, felt underused and flabby. And I'm not looking for Twinkies to nourish my soul.

But I don't want gruel, either. Though they stand at opposite ends of the religious spectrum, ultra-Orthodox Judaism has much in common with the Renewal movement. In its rejection of most of the major ideas of the Enlightenment, ultra-Orthodoxy has adopted a shtetl mentality and structure, closing itself off from the modern world by living in insular enclaves either carved out of urban areas (such as Brooklyn) or far removed in the country (as in the Catskills). While not necessarily as emotionally open as the Renewal crowd, ultra-Orthodox Jews can be just as anti-intellectual, yet in a radically different way. Their literalist, black-and-white approach to Judaism leaves no room, in any meaningful sense, for critical thought and mindful exploration. As religious fundamentalists, they don't think—they absorb.

Both of these groups, regardless of denomination, offer responses to the problems of contemporary Judaism.

Both responses stink. And none of the other mainstream Jewish denominations have offered much better.

The Renewal movement gives us more heart, but at the expense of our head; ultra-Orthodoxy lets us keep our head, but limits it to serving as a sponge for the infallible truths it dictates. Yet our brain is not, and never has been, the enemy. The enemy is the way in which, for the last couple of centuries, we've granted reason and rationality absolute primacy over all of the other elements that constitute the whole human being. Our era now cries out for something different and new, something far more difficult to achieve—a balance of head *and* heart.

We need "hybrid" models of Jewish life, models that allow for the healthy coexistence and creative interplay of intellect and emotion. And by emotion I'm not talking about superficial, vapid exuberance, but authentic, real feeling—deep, complex, and heartfelt.

That's not as easy as it sounds. As much as I love my own congregation, The New Shul, getting our members to simply put their hands together and clap during worship services (forget about dancing in the aisles) is often like extracting molars—and I'm the rabbi emeritus of a congregation in Greenwich Village, New York, a neighborhood that serves as a symbol (or at least used to) of free, open, uninhibited expression. It's frustrated the hell out of me. I've actually stopped services on occasion and, lovingly, chastised our community, urging them to get out of their skulls and into their guts, their kishkes, if they ever expect the prayers to do anything for them.

Religion is something you have to experience concretely and directly. It isn't an abstract, ethereal idea, nor is it a "thing" that you gaze at from a distance with wonderment or incredulity, like you would the Grand Canyon or a bearded lady. At its best, religion is not only accessible, but a force that flows through your entire body, from your nerve endings to your cerebellum.

It is something that you live.

One of the hybrid models that my community and others have adopted successfully, a model that is both experiential and alive, is the Hasidic *tish*. In the Yiddish language, *tish* translates simply as "table," but in the spiritual context it means much more. The origin of the *tish* ritual is murky (it goes back at least two centuries), yet even now, modern-day Hasidic men still gather around long tables to drink, eat, sing, and listen to words of wisdom and inspiration from their rebbes, their rabbinic gurus. These joyous—and sometimes rowdy—occasions are usually held on festivals or on Saturdays near dusk, at the end of Shabbat.

But you don't have to be Hasidic, or male, to hold a *tish*. You don't even need a synagogue (though they can serve as boilerplates to build from). All you need is a group of friends, a knowledgeable leader, and a chilled bottle of vodka.

Since my fiercely independent congregation is not affiliated with any established denomination or ideology, we feel absolutely free to draw from both progressive innovations as well as from earlier, even discarded or arcane, Jewish practices. Some of our religious events and observances are more traditional than you'd find in a typical liberal synagogue, while others are avant-garde and experimental (more on some of those, both in my shul and in others, later). Through both our name and our approach to Judaism, we've strived hard to create a community that harmonizes not only the head and the heart but the old and the new.

The Hasidic *tish* has given us one such opportunity. Yet we have taken this traditional structure and given it a downtown edge. A *tish* at The New Shul may still take place around a table, and it may still occur at dusk on the eve of a festival or on a Saturday night, but it is far different in nature from a *tish* you'd find in Brooklyn or Bnei Brak (an ultra-Orthodox enclave in Israel). Though, as our shul's founding rabbi, I've usually led the *tish,* I've never been treated like a guru. Rather than sitting passively and listening to my

self-indulgent ramblings, my community has actively engaged me in dialogue—and it has often gotten raucous and
heated. My reaction? *Bring it on.* I've tossed out a provocative
idea (such as whether Judaism can exist without a belief in
God) or passed out a controversial text (on, for example, the
various and sometimes conflicting Jewish views on evil), and
then we've mixed it up. Our own version of the *tish* is egalitarian, interactive, nonhierarchical, passionate.

It's a kind of dance. At times it's more of a brawl.

But it is always as soulful as it is intellectual. Our discussion
may function as the centerpiece of the *tish,* but it is circum-
scribed by singing. Ellen Gould, our musical director and co-
founder, generally leads the table in a variety of *niggunim,* or
wordless melodies—Hasidic creations that are highly accessible and participatory. Some of the *niggunim* that Ellen chooses
are warm and uplifting; some convey blues and longing. And
when you add booze and food to this mystical concoction, you
get a powerful ritual that feeds the heart and mind simultaneously. The *tish* isn't a formal service, and it isn't a campfire
sing-along. Yet it is always life affirming and spirit moving, always an experience.

It's just that experiential component that is the key to re-
suscitating contemporary Jewish life. Men and women in today's society, including Jews, want to do and experience
things for themselves—take a look at the enormous commercial success of companies like Home Depot and Ikea, or
the explosive growth of the exotic and adventure travel in-
dustries. The same is true in the realm of religion. We're
tired of being "Jews in the Pews," of being talked at as if we
were an audience in an academic lecture hall. Many of us are
tired of sitting in the pews altogether.

So let's examine another hands-on, hybrid example of Jewish practice, but one that is far more individualistic in form

and focus. I find myself yet again turning to the classical Hasidic mystical tradition, to a ritual developed and refined two centuries ago by Rabbi Nachman of Breslov, a spiritual master who knew firsthand the inner poles of light and dark, as well as the shadowy regions in between, of the human psyche. The practice is called *hitbodedut,* and it is best translated as "self-seclusion" or "self-isolation."

The basic idea behind this ritual, which originated as a solitary practice, is very simple: In a private, preferably natural setting, we address God directly. Removed from the formal context and liturgy of the synagogue, and from the company of other people, we express to our Creator—using our own thoughts or words—whatever it is that is going on inside us. We can "converse," pray, plead, confess, repent, cry, meditate. For this practice to work, all we really need are open minds and open hearts. Any emotional expression or feeling will do— whether it be joy, gratitude, serenity, or frustration, doubt, even anger. Reb Nachman says that during *hitbodedut,* we can even pray for the *ability* to pray. This highly personal practice is a totally unique experience for everyone, and it depends entirely on what an individual is going through as well as how vulnerable and honest that person is willing to be.

I've led *hitbodedut* exercises for synagogues, universities, and retreat centers, and I never know what to expect. Age doesn't matter. Geography doesn't matter. Nothing seems to matter but the state of a person's soul.

When we all return from the practice at a predetermined time, from our nooks and crannies in the woods and fields— our private sanctuaries where, as Reb Nachman says, "the grass will awaken your heart"—I ask those who have participated to share what their experience was like with the rest of the group. Sometimes they say it was life changing, and that it allowed them to access and reveal secret places of struggle and pain that had been festering in their hearts; other times participants have just sat on tree stumps and watched the clouds go by. I've seen some weep, while others smirked.

One of my like-minded colleagues and somebody not afraid to push boundaries is Rabbi Mordecai Finley, the spiritual leader of Congregation Ohr HaTorah in Los Angeles and a former marine. Finley has incorporated *hitbodedut* into his personal observance with a regularity that makes me jealous. Maybe it's because of his challenging experiences "out in the field" back when he was a jarhead that Finley grasps, probably better than most, the raw, elemental power of this Hasidic ritual, a ritual that blends self-reflection with self-expression. Finley—like other rabbis I know—is convinced that *hitbodedut* makes him a better religious teacher, but that it also takes him out of the world of mainstream Judaism. And he couldn't give a damn.

What on earth could be more gonzo than standing toe-to-toe with God and laying it all on the line—or wandering through the woods talking, crying, shouting, laughing, and swearing? Best of all, we can practice *hitbodedut* spontaneously and independently, anytime, anywhere, and with absolutely no prerequisites.

What *is* mainstream Judaism, and why am I—just like Finley—so much more comfortable on the fringes? I don't think I can come up with anything that better epitomizes the mainstream, as well as what is deeply disturbing about Judaism in this country, than American bar and bat mitzvahs.

They're fiascoes. What were once joyful but relatively minor rites of passage for young Jews have become ends in themselves, virtually secularized religious events neutered of most of their spiritual content and focused on all the wrong things. Rather than functioning as gateways to our faith, they are treated by too many parents—and, ultimately, transmitted to their children—as exits from it. Rather than being viewed as just one of many high points in the course of their lifelong Jewish journeys, they are seen as climactic conclusions to them.

Synagogues fail because they mostly acquiesce to this mind-set in order to hold on to their members. Religious school training in the year before the Big Day often focuses almost exclusively on the ceremony itself, on the rote memorization of prayers and Torah verses rather than on a serious, exciting exploration of Judaism. Parents fail because they generally offer zero support at home, frequently undermining the synagogue's intermittent attempts to change things (as was the case with one father I worked with, who kept telling his son that "it's almost over," as if the bar mitzvah process was like passing a kidney stone). Parents also fail because of all the energy, time, money, and importance they put into their postservice parties, materialistic bashes that turn celebrations into desecrations. When I was a student rabbi, one child's parents actually brought in elephants and had a circus tent erected for the occasion. Elephants—in *Montana*.

And we wonder why we're not touching our children's souls, why they suddenly vanish from our congregations before they turn fourteen.

The late Arnold Jacob Wolf, rabbi emeritus of K.A.M. Isaiah Israel Congregation in Chicago, was a mentor of mine and a provocateur extraordinaire. While he was an older man, he was definitely not old school in his attitude. In his decades of social activism and service to the Jewish community, Wolf had seen and heard it all—the good, the bad, the ugly, and the even uglier. He wasn't one to hold back his words once he unleashed them. "The modern bar and bat mitzvah," Wolf argued, "is a truly dangerous thing. It communicates narcissism instead of obligation. It's the worship of the child, instead of the child's worship of God. If that's not a kind of idolatry, what is?"

So how do we treat our kids as human beings instead of idols? How do we touch them in their hearts and souls? And how do we make parents get it?

One strategy that Wolf and other rabbis and congregations have utilized is to require the bar or bat mitzvah student to commit for a year—with his or her family—to a service project. That could mean, to highlight just a few of the many examples, helping a blind person learn how to read, grocery shopping for a housebound elderly person, or working at an overnight shelter for the homeless. Why add this specific activity to the bar and bat mitzvah requirements? In order to give the process more perspective and teeth, to help the student and family get beyond their own world of narrow self-concern and begin to reach and try to repair the fractured world around them.

In my own community, I've tried to take that approach a step further. I don't think ethical commitments are enough. You can learn what it means to be a good person but still remain ignorant about what it means to be a good Jew—moral behavior is a necessary but insufficient condition for being a fully actualized member of the Jewish people. Christians and Muslims are also charged by their respective faith traditions to care for the poor and needy. It is in the area of religious particularism, not universalism—the observance of communion, for instance, or the making of a pilgrimage to Mecca—that makes a Christian a Christian and a Muslim a Muslim. So, in addition to the community service obligation, I've required that all of our bar and bat mitzvah students commit to a ritual practice as well.

Some students have commited to keeping some form of *kashrut,* or dietary observance, during the course of their preparatory year; some have decided to light Shabbat candles on Friday nights and to say the attendant blessings over wine and challah; other children have chosen to recite the *Sh'ma* prayer, the quintessential Jewish declaration of monotheistic belief, before they go to bed and then again when they wake up. What they do after their bar or bat mitzvah ceremony is their business, and I've told them that—that's the whole point, making educated decisions, as mature Jews, about Judaism and Jewish observance. But I want their decisions to be rooted in experience and experimentation, not ignorance. I want them to actually *feel* what it's like to say a blessing before eating a meal, to *practice* a particular ritual or rite, rather than just read about it in a textbook.

And, wonder of wonders, it seems to be working. Kids are smarter than we adults often give them credit for, and they don't mind being challenged—after all, at their ages, they have coaches and tutors who challenge them all the time, and I think they genuinely appreciate it. Through this system the parents support, and monitor, their child's ethical and ritual commitments. The ceremony, while still a focus of more concern than I wish it were, has shifted (ever so slightly) from the foreground to the background.

When the Big Day eventually arrives, the joy somehow feels much more organic and natural, and the celebration more profound and authentic.

Judaism is not just about what happens in the synagogue. And the expression of Jewish identity, religious or otherwise, doesn't have to be solemn and subdued. The days of the huge, German-Jewish temples—and of the associated decorum, formality, and reserve of the Jews who built and attended them—are, or ought to be, long gone. Though there remain some throwbacks to those "high church" institutions and attitudes, they'll die out in a generation, guaranteed. They have to. As our society becomes more and more decentralized, so must its organs of religion. Judaism can and often should be taken out of the sanctuary and into the home, the streets, the public square. Judaism needs to meet us where we are—and most of us aren't in synagogue very often.

Some scholars think that, partly in reaction to the Enlightenment and its rationalistic, repressive, Protestant, bourgeois sensibility, Jewish identity has been inextricably linked in modern times with an intense urge to act out, to rebel against rules, codes, formality, civility, authority. Sometimes that urge has been suppressed. Sometimes it's been sublimated into an impulse to assimilate, as we see in many of those involved in the old-school temples mentioned above. But frequently, and in truly outrageous ways, the revolt against these forces has led to tremendous creativity and innovation in the sciences and arts.

Take Freud's revolutionary ideas in the field of psychology. Or Marx in the area of economics. Or Einstein's rebellion against the way we think about time and space. Or look instead at popular culture, particularly comedy. Who do you find among its classic figures? The Marx Brothers and the Three Stooges—groups of audacious Jewish men who turn highbrow society completely upside down. Nearly every plot involves some pretentious, snooty party at a mansion, or a stuffy evening at the opera, or a staid and boring journey aboard a fancy cruise ship—all of which are absolutely ruined by men acting like buffoons in order to show who the real buffoons are. Below the surface, the urge to overturn, overwhelm, and overcome is a distinctly *Jewish* urge. It might not be overtly religious, but it is real and right in your face.

Still, our gonzo Jewish spirits sometimes need an infusion of, well, spirits. In keeping with the Hasidic tradition of blending head and heart, religious inquiry and corporeal pleasure, our congregation created a wildly successful program called Spirits & Spirituality. In a hip, casual, downtown Manhattan bar, The New Shul held, over the course of several evenings, stimulating—and refreshing—adult education sessions with names like Kabbalah & Cosmopolitans and Mussar & Mojitos. While I led the discussions on various Jewish spiritual movements, one of our religious school teachers, a young actress who was also a professional bartender, mixed the drinks.

Some of the participants—members who I'd usually see only a couple of times a year, during the High Holy Days—stayed until closing.

Our Spirits & Spirituality program was an outgrowth of a parallel activity that had emerged spontaneously at our synagogue's annual retreat, where, on Friday night after dinner and services, the kids would go to sleep and the adults would gather around a table to essentially play drinking games—but with a more mature, spiritual twist. We decided, "What the hell, let's create an entire series using this model, and let's open it to the public." We're not alone. Others have sponsored similar programs, combining the urban passion for boozing it up with an interest in things intellectual and esoteric. A group called Tribeca Hebrew held several events that paired different wines with different aspects of Jewish mysticism: Zohar & Zinfandel, Sefirot & Syrah, Cosmos & Cabernet.

In-your-face audacity. Taking it to the streets. Informality. Merging head and heart. These have been some of the guiding principles of the new Judaism that many Jews, especially the younger generation of Jewish leaders, have been following in our ongoing quest to find—or construct—a revitalized faith. At its best religion can be the greatest of adventures, opening doors to mysteries and marvels beyond comprehension, beyond even good and evil. The Hebrew word for holiness, *kedushah,* implies "otherness," something that transcends the world of the ordinary, the world of rational, definable categories. When we enter holy space or time, wherever or whenever that may be, we should feel as if we've entered a different plane, a different zone of existence and experience. Our Judaism, if it is to be dynamic and profound, needs to *transport* us.

But unless they are continuously reviewed and renewed, the tiresome repetition of prayers and traditions can be paralyzing, not transporting. And when, as is the case so often today, we're told by the Jewish establishment to observe our heritage through messages of fear and insecurity—told to be Jewish, for example, not because Judaism is beautiful, but because, as some have argued, we don't want to give Hitler a posthumous victory—then that paralysis can mutate into loathing. When I was younger and less thoughtful about these matters I sort of liked the concept of being Jewish out of spite, as a defiant statement to the world and to history that we haven't been beaten yet.

Now the idea makes me sick.

Judaism ought to be based on fun, not fear. It ought to be enjoyable. Though our spiritual tradition is certainly about obligations and duties, it is also about celebration. As the biblical writer Kohelet said more than two millennia ago (and as Pete Seeger echoed much later through song), "For everything there is a season, a time for every experience under heaven." The twentieth century, for Jews and others, was a winter of discontent. I want this new century to be a spring of satisfaction.

In the cycle of Jewish holidays, one of the most audacious, fun, and ultimately satisfying is the spring festival of Purim. For hundreds of years, and in diverse communities all over the globe, we've acted out this biblical, mythic story of triumph— of the Jews in Persia over those who would oppress and kill them, of the heroic Esther over her enemies in the royal court, of the wise Mordechai over the wicked Haman.

These rambunctious community dramas are known as Purim *shpils*. Not insignificantly, Purim is the only Jewish holiday during which we are actually commanded to consume alcohol. Many have called it a Jewish Mardi Gras, when everything becomes topsy-turvy: Men dress like women, women dress like men, and not only does religion suddenly become fun, but *we* become the center of the action.

We need more of our religious festivals and services to feel like Purim, not just because of its celebratory nature, but because it places all of us at center stage. Observers are turned into actors; congregants become clerics. And we need Purim itself to stay as brazen and radical as ever—if not grow more so. Popular culture has much to teach us in this area. When my community wanted to produce a *shpil* that pushed the envelope a little further than the norm, we held a discussion on what our goals for the event were. We wanted it to be interactive and intergenerational. We wanted everyone present to be a participant in the drama. We also wanted to flesh out the complex role of Esther and demonstrate her protofeminism more clearly. And we wanted it to be an in-your-face experience—provocative, confrontational, raw.

I wrote the script, based on the ancient biblical scroll, with our cofounders (both of whom are professional writers). It was pretty good, but we needed a punchy title that fit the event. At the time, the controversial theatrical piece *The Vagina Monologues* was a huge national hit. We decided that if Esther had been alive today, she'd have been one of the voices in the show. And so, *The Hamantaschen Monologues* was born. Hamantaschen, or "Haman's Ears," are triangular fruit-filled cookies eaten on Purim and shaped as if Georgia O'Keeffe had kneaded them in her own kitchen.

With the active participation of our shul's artists and de-
signers we created a space that looked and felt like a fantastical
party at a Persian palace: Courtesans and royal guards (congregational members in character) roamed the hall in flowing
gowns and chain mail; musicians, some seated on a dais and
some strolling around the room, played their various instruments; court jesters clowned with the kids; food and drink sat
lavishly on long tables. When you entered our space you
weren't just watching a party—you were a guest *at* the party,
which is how the scroll of Esther actually begins. There was no
boundary that separated the biblical story from the people in
the room. As our interpretation of the Purim drama unfolded,
everyone who was present had a role in it, even if they hadn't
known ahead of time. Adults and children alike understood
what we were trying to do. They knew that they weren't pas-
sive observers attending a sacred ritual, but that they themselves had become part of one.

Our Purim *shpil* raised some eyebrows—but it also raised
some spirits and, I hope, the bar for reimagining Jewish ritual.

There is no magic potion that will turn today's Jews on to Judaism. What is clear is that if we give our ancient faith a second chance—a chance it deserves, since Judaism itself
shouldn't be blamed for our distortions of it—there are several
core areas in Jewish life that must be changed: accessibility to
our faith, even for those on the "outside" who are looking in;
the tone and feel of our worship; the ways in which we present
and frame our opportunities for learning; the false and un-
healthy dichotomy that exists between mind and heart; the focus on fear-motivated activities rather than experiential,
transporting happenings that slug us in the gut.

Good writing teachers often say to their students: "Show,
don't tell." It's an approach we in the Jewish community

should follow. Nobody's going to become an active, committed Jew in this age and culture if we simply try to convince
them to, whatever the arguments we might use; they're going
to buy into Jewish life only if what they see is something that
they *want* to be a part of. The power of Jewish ritual, once it is
unshackled from the chains we've trapped it in, can speak for
itself. We need to stop our damn whining, set it free, and let it
rock our world.

CHAPTER 2

Extreme (*Not* Extremist) Religion

THE WINDS WEREN'T GALE FORCE, but they were strong enough to make striking my matches nearly impossible. And with the midnight sun hanging like a dim bulb directly in front of us, it was hard to determine what exactly constituted a genuine sunset. Still, it was late on a Friday, and even though we were standing on Icy Reef, a band of small islands that forms a fragile barrier between the Alaskan mainland and the Arctic Ocean, I was trying to help our group usher in a midsummer Shabbat with a pair of candles.

"Come on, Rabbi," said one of the trip's more grizzled participants. (We'd been sea kayaking for almost a week.) "Can't you use your special connection to God to stop these gusts and get those things lit? I'm ready for dinner!"

"Aha!" I responded. "You've just unwittingly given us our spiritual teaching for the day. You know, it was only *after* Job learned to face the uncontrollable whirlwind with patience and resignation that his true reward finally came."

"You're not going to get all religious on us, are you? Not right here, not at the edge of the world?"

"You're damn right I am, you rabble-rousing Heeb," I answered. "That's why we came up here in the first place!"

And that was no lie. With the help of my friend Dave, who ran a Fairbanks-based travel company called Arctic Wild, I'd gathered a small group—some from my young synagogue in Manhattan, some who had no link whatsoever to organized Jewish life—to join me on a Jewish Outward Bound adventure in the high Arctic. On this trip, we'd interweave the physical challenges of sea kayaking and backcountry hiking and camping with the spiritual and moral lessons of Judaism, using texts from the Bible, the Talmud, and mysticism as our teaching tools—along with nature itself.

We would also practice "religion in the raw" by observing a Sabbath on the North Slope of the Arctic National Wildlife Refuge.

Nobody present had had a positive experience in Hebrew school as a kid. Nobody, not even the members of my congregation, attended services regularly. Yet there we all were on Icy Reef, a quorum of Jews in thermals and fleece, braced against the frigid winds of the Beaufort Sea, celebrating the ancient holy day of Shabbat with light, wine, and bread (though we had to bless tasteless hardtack crackers instead of braided loaves of sweet challah). When the banter subsided, something about that place made Shabbat feel more real and Judaism more alive.

We were affirming the moment of Creation in the very heart of creation.

"This sure isn't the Judaism they taught me growing up," someone else said. "If it was, I'd never have left it."

Though we discussed the same sacred texts, practiced the same age-old rites, and engaged in the same kind of community building and bonding that our forebears had done for centuries, it was the *context* in which we did these things that made all the difference, that transformed our trip's participants' disaffection toward Judaism into an affection for a religious tradition that they'd previously written off.

Judaism itself hadn't changed. But its presentation had— and in radical, even playful ways.

Religious extremism is a monstrous thing. The World Trade Center attacks of September 11, 2001, and the faith-based violence that continues to roil our world, make that fact all too clear. Having worked as a law-enforcement chaplain at Ground Zero in the immediate aftermath of the terror attacks, I witnessed the effects of this grotesque impulse firsthand. I remember the sight of utter devastation: the wasteland of smashed buildings and shattered windows; fantastic, hideous pillars of twisted steel; plumes of smoke rising eerily from the rubble.

Yet "extreme" religion is a different animal altogether, and it can be just as exciting, powerful, and personally transformative as extreme sports.

What's the difference between these two forms of religious expression? An extremist approach to religion closes a person's mind and makes that person subservient to and radicalized about a particular set of (usually distorted and warped) doctrines and beliefs. An extreme approach to religious life is about keeping one's mind *open,* about experimenting with bold and unconventional techniques for transmitting spiritual knowledge and for reshaping souls.

Extremist religion breeds suicide bombers; extreme religion leads to self-empowerment.

But extreme religion scares the crap out of normative religion. Why? Because it calls into question, by its sheer existence, the supposed value of the comfort and security that is offered by a more conventional, bourgeois approach to religious life.

It also calls into question its necessity.

If a Jewish man has to travel all the way to the Arctic Ocean in order to have the kind of intense religious experience that he never had in synagogue, it speaks as poorly of Judaism's current institutions as it does positively about the religion's transcendent—and portable—character. And if a Jewish woman can ride the rapids in Patagonia while simultaneously intensifying her spiritual identity and increasing her religious knowledge, how can a formal lecture at the local Jewish Community Center (JCC) ever appeal to her again?

Extreme religion is lean and mean. It offers challenge rather than comfort, risk rather than conservatism.

It is about pushing boundaries, not constructing them.

And it is a growing phenomenon. While the adventure travel and leadership training fields have understood for some time how much men and women in our culture crave the deep sense of satisfaction, and spirituality, that often come with facing and overcoming obstacles—as well as the inspiration of the outdoors—religion has been a relative latecomer to what is, in essence, a kind of party for the human spirit.

But it's catching on. Many groups, both organized and informal, have emerged from within—and sometimes from without—the Jewish community, groups that strive to incorporate into core Jewish teachings the techniques and tools of experienced secular organizations such as Outward Bound and NOLS (the National Outdoor Leadership School) in order to foster Jewish identity and literacy.

Nature, the classroom for these endeavors, often plays a key role—but not an exclusive one. At least as important, if not more so, is the presence of some sort of physical challenge: kayaking, caving, rock climbing.

Yet it is a physical challenge designed for a *meta*physical purpose.

If a buttoned-down corporation like IBM can broaden its thinking and get its employees to develop self-confidence through the use of ropes challenge courses, and if Pepsi can have its personnel learn about the importance of teamwork by taking them on canoe trips, we in the Jewish world would be absolute idiots if we thought that Jews, especially younger ones, wouldn't be drawn to similar programs to learn about Jewish ethical and spiritual values—if only we made them accessible and readily available all over the country, not just in pockets of creativity here and there.

Those pockets do exist. One of the first people in professional Jewish life to recognize the utility and power of nature-based extreme religion was Rabbi Howard Cohen. In 1990, Cohen created Burning Bush Adventures as a side project while he was a seminarian at the Reconstructionist Rabbinical College. A former Outward Bound instructor and program director, his goal was to blend outdoor adventure with Jewish living and learning. In 1994, when Cohen became the spiritual leader of Congregation Beth El in Bennington, Vermont, he brought Burning Bush with him.

Since Burning Bush's founding, Cohen has led high school, college, and graduate students, as well as individuals and families, on trips throughout New England's mountains, forests, lakes, and rivers. On occasion, Cohen leads trips to Israel as well. They can involve outdoor physical activities as moderate as hiking and cross-country skiing or as grueling as dogsledding and ice climbing.

Though Cohen's synagogue is affiliated with the Reconstructionist movement, his trips do not impose a denominational bias. In order to make every Burning Bush experience accessible and attractive to Jews of all religious (or nonreligious) stripes, meals are vegetarian, time is always allotted for personal as well as group prayer, and special sensitivity is made on Shabbat toward participants who come from a more traditional background. "Our goal with Burning Bush," says Cohen, "is to facilitate an authentic Jewish experience in the wilderness, not to promote a particular kind of Judaism. My ultimate objective is to have Jews redefine their relationship with the world around and within them, and Judaism is a part of both."

There is a quote from rabbinic literature on the home page of Burning Bush's Web site: "Whoever would wish to acquire Torah must make himself ownerless like the wilderness." This fifteen-hundred-year-old teaching could serve as the mission statement for many of the groups and individuals in this chapter. But what does it mean to be "ownerless," to be the possession of no one or thing? It means that like the wilderness you stand apart, disconnected, cut off—yet also open in that emptiness. Many contemporary Jews feel cut off, detached from Judaism and Jewish life. For one ancient sage, though, that is precisely the place we ought to begin our spiritual journey.

We can't really appreciate or possess the riches of our religious heritage until we've first experienced the poverty and yearning of a life without them.

My friend Bob Greenbaum and I had that same outreach idea in mind—the idea of reaching Jews on the religious periphery—when, in 1998, we started Jewish Adventure Travel. At the time Bob was the owner and operator of Uprising, the nation's largest outdoor rock-climbing facility, located in Palm Springs and close to Joshua Tree National Park, a mecca for rock climbers and the laboratory for some of our trial trips. I was working in Manhattan as a teaching fellow at a think tank, CLAL: The National Jewish Center for Learning and Leadership. David Elcott, then CLAL's executive vice president, knew about my love of adventure travel and that I'd just come back from a dogsledding trip in Alaska. Elcott thought that Bob and I should meet, since Bob had similar interests and also happened to be a CLAL board member. We met a month later to brainstorm about how we might join forces.

My goal was both professional and personal—I wanted to reach alienated Jews and turn them on to Judaism, but I also wanted to harmonize, in my own soul, the call of the wild and the call of my faith.

Bob had a somewhat different agenda. He wanted to connect in a deeper, more experiential way with his Jewish roots. "As an adult," Bob says, "I wanted to be challenged and to challenge others to explore their own limitations, using Judaism and the outdoors to tap into our humanity."

In the spring of 1999 Bob and I met with the Jewish community in Las Vegas and organized a rock-climbing excursion into Red Rock Canyon, Nevada, for a dozen high school students and their teachers. The participants came from the city's various synagogues, and many of them, we were told, were not very enthusiastic about their religious education programs.

Our job was to give them fresh inspiration.

We hiked to the site with our gear, and before attempting our first ascent we went over all of the basics: how to tie a proper knot; how to communicate with your partner on the other end of the rope; how to climb; how to descend. Then I shared an old Hasidic parable about teamwork and told the group how vital it was that each of us learn to trust one another from that point forward. It was community building, not touching the top of some lifeless mountain face, that was the true mission of our day.

Once in a tropical country, a certain splendid bird, more col-orful than any that had ever been seen, was sighted at the top of the tallest tree. The bird's plumage contained within it all the colors in the world. But the bird was perched so high that no single person could ever hope to reach it. When news of the bird reached the ears of the king, he ordered that a number of men try to bring the bird to him. They were to stand on one another's shoulders until the highest man could reach the bird and bring it to the king. The men assembled near the tree, but while they were standing balanced on one another's shoulders, some of those near the bottom decided to wander off. As soon as the first man moved, the entire chain collapsed, injuring several of the men. Still the bird re-mained uncaptured. The men had doubly failed the king. For even greater than his desire to see the bird was his wish to see his people so closely joined to one another.

Despite this parable—or perhaps because of it—every single student present successfully climbed to the summit of the moderately difficult 5.7-rated trail. Many of them, especially the younger and less confident ones, scrambled their way up the cliff for a few feet, struggled to find new ledges for their feet or fingers, and then shouted that they couldn't climb any higher and wanted to give up. But with a little prodding from either me, Bob, or a peer, the student would eventually muster the courage and climb higher and higher until he or she reached the top. When the students rappelled back down to the ground, the look on their faces was one of joyful exhilaration, and the sense of accomplishment that emanated from them was palpable and almost overwhelming.

After our climb and at the base of the rock wall, I passed out a sheet of paper to each participant as we sat together in a tight circle. Printed on it was a famous aphorism from Hillel, the ancient Jewish sage: "If I am not for myself, who will be for me? If I am only for myself, what am I? If not now, when?" Using that text and the fresh memory of—and scrapes from—our respective climbs, I led a discussion on our individual experiences and on the key role that the values of initiative, interdependence, and motivation played in them. In the course of our spirited conversation I tried to make a few basic points:

- *Nobody's going to climb that rock face for you—you've got to do it yourself.*

- *You're a fool unless you're connected to someone else, and you're immoral if you don't pay attention to the needs of your partner.*

- *What are you waiting for? Move your Jewish ass and get to the damn top!*

I showed how those values weren't just modern and secular, but deep-rooted and Jewish. Everybody was receptive and seemed to grasp what was going on. Having just confronted and surmounted their own physical challenges, our group nodded in agreement as I explained how each one of those core values could be applied well beyond rock climbing in the desert to the more commonplace challenges in our everyday lives at home, as well as to our communities.

"You mean all this old Jewish stuff can relate to the real world?" one student asked me.

"Darn right, Junior."

"This is a lot more cool than learning about it in a classroom," the boy went on. The teachers smiled awkwardly.

"Look around us," I said. "We *are* in a classroom."

All that Bob and I had done was to frame the experience of rock climbing in a specifically Jewish way. In the process, though, we'd tuned in and attracted a group of young Jews to their spiritual tradition and demonstrated, with the beauty of nature and an exciting outdoor activity as teaching tools, just how relevant and inspiring their (formerly irrelevant and boring) religion could actually be.

Jews are often shocked the first time they're exposed to traditional Jewish teachings that convey ideas or values that seem so contemporary and even . . . hip. How could bespectacled, bearded, bookish rabbis (that seems to be our unfortunate caricature these days) have known so long ago about the raw, primal power of nature? How could those seemingly dull and out-of-touch sages have grasped how frightening and difficult human experience can sometimes be?

Did those dudes ever go rock climbing?

I don't know whether any of our rabbinic forebears had climbing shoes or carabiners, but I do know that they fully fathomed the capacity of nature to elevate and transform souls if we'd only view it from the right perspective.

Those teachers are dead and buried, but their teachings can—and must—live on. Despite this cultural climate, where we want everything handed to us without our having to work for it, the burden is on *us* to rediscover their insights and wisdom.

To borrow the mantra from *The X-Files,* "The truth is out there."

Can we handle the truth, let alone grow from it? Sure, but for that to happen we need to be exposed to it. And since the Jewish mainstream, in its mind-boggling myopia, has yet to adequately support or promote the kinds of programs and groups that this chapter is about (groups with target audiences of hungry, disconnected Jews who would probably only set foot in an actual synagogue once in a blue moon), all that most of us often have to work with are words.

But words can change worlds. That's what makes a gonzo

approach to Judaism such a countercultural and affirmative statement: It offers a bold, brash alternative to the prevalent trends in both American *and* Jewish institutional life.

Nature, and our relationship to it, is at the core of Jewish identity. And since so many people I've encountered through my work as a cleric testify to how some of their most spiritual and life-changing experiences have taken place in the context of nature, I've done my best, through my writing and my teaching, to bring to the surface what Judaism has to say about the matter. When we know we're not alone, we feel more comfortable. And when we know that our religion is in sync with our own views, then it makes us that much more connected to and comfortable with it.

The truth may be out there, but it is also in here, waiting for us, embedded in the faith that is our inheritance and gift. Roughly two centuries ago Rabbi Schneur Zalman of Lyady, the founder of today's Chabad-Lubavitch movement, wrote the following: "All that we see—the heaven, the earth, and all that fills them—all these things are but the external garments of God."

Now that's radical. While Schneur Zalman isn't saying that nature is God (that would be pantheism, not the monotheism of Judaism), he is saying that the stars, the seas, and the forests—as well as the birds in the sky and the beasts of the field—are, in Jewish reality, far more than they appear. They are the outer clothing of the divine, the coat of many colors that cloaks the world's Creator. Regardless of what many modern Jews think (or have been told), Judaism does recognize the face behind the mask, the God that is revealed to us not in bricks-and-mortar synagogues, but in the *natural* sanctuaries of deserts, oceans, and mountain ranges. That is the God many of us know more intimately, and those are the sanctuaries where many of us feel more comfortable.

Our sages may not have been active rock climbers, but they clearly understood how nature holds a sacred power that is often hidden from our daily sight.

While words can change worlds, action is frequently more effective. Jewish Adventure Travel no longer exists. Although Bob and I failed to maintain our company, we gave it our best shot, and it was well worth the effort. I still run customized outdoor trips on my own, intermittently, as people or organizations request my services (with more and more of my trips being geared toward college students). Fortunately for the wider Jewish community, however, there are other start-up groups now on the scene that are trying to fill the void—but that continue to contend with many of the same issues that we did. One such group is TorahTrek.

In 1996, Mike Comins was a freshly minted rabbi, having just been ordained at the Jerusalem campus of Hebrew Union College–Jewish Institute of Religion (my religious alma mater). Though he was about to begin a doctoral program and was writing about God in Israel, "I felt like my soul had been choked off," he recalls. Comins had spent much of his childhood hiking through the Sierra Nevada mountains in California, and so, in the face of his disillusionment and confusion, he did what he'd always done—he loaded up his backpack and headed into the wilderness.

"That trip into the Sinai desert changed everything," Comins says. "All this theology was in my head, but it took walking in the desert for me to really feel God in my heart. I realized that I was closer to God in the wilderness than in words." After that experience—an experience that helped him to explore the link between his "inner and outer geography"— Comins decided to earn a license as an Israeli desert guide. He founded *Ruach ha-Midbar* ("Spirit of the Desert") and spent

the next two years leading spiritual treks and retreats in the
Negev and Sinai deserts and mountains, counting rabbis, rabbinical students, and Christian seminarians among his diverse
trip participants.

When Comins returned to the United States he brought
his concept with him, and eventually established TorahTrek:
Spiritual Wilderness Adventures. Since 2001, Comins has
been leading groups on treks and retreats primarily in the
western region of the country, in places like California,
Wyoming, Colorado, Arizona, and New Mexico. Sometimes
he customizes a trip for a group of individuals; other times he
partners with another Jewish organization or synagogue. On
all of his spiritual adventures, however, Comins interweaves
Jewish texts with hiking, kayaking, and other outdoor activities to convey his insights on personal spirituality and environmental ethics.

But here's the rub, and it's a big and damn irritating one:
As effective as TorahTrek and Burning Bush are, they lack
the financial and administrative resources to cast a wider net
and touch more lives. Comins and Cohen are essentially on
their own, as were Bob and I. While the Jewish establishment
has made back-to-nature outings a fixture of children's summer camps for a long time, it has yet to fully comprehend how
meaningful these programs can be for *adults*. And so these
bold initiatives frequently founder. Many, like ours, have gone
under completely.

As long as this kind of extreme religion remains unsup-
ported by our national institutions, its life-altering power will
reach very few people, and it will never expand beyond tiny
niche segments of the Jewish community. Still, younger, visionary rabbis, educators, and entrepreneurs aren't waiting
around. Some Jewish outdoor adventure groups are trying to
branch into the more traditionalist and even Orthodox camps

(Kosher Expeditions, Teva Adventure, and Koshertreks are a few examples) in order to expose as many people as possible, including the very observant, to the marvels of religious adventures both in North America as well as in exotic locales around the world.

Some proponents of religion in the raw have chosen to focus their energy and expertise not primarily in the areas of Jewish education or identity development, but rather in religious life-cycle events. The men and women who run these groups arrange for rabbinic or other clerical supervision and officiation at spiritual rites of passage such as bar and bat mitzvahs, weddings, baby namings, conversions, and the like—all within the context of a beautiful outdoor environment.

Like many others who've created Jewish adventure programs, Rabbi Jamie Korngold wanted to forge a rabbinate where her two loves—Judaism and nature—would work in tandem. While serving as a pulpit rabbi in Alberta, Canada, Korngold was asked by a couple who were not members of a congregation to officiate at their adopted baby's conversion and naming. Korngold jumped at the opportunity. The beautiful, private ceremony was held in a canyon, and, in 2001, a model for Adventure Rabbi was established. Korngold left her position in Calgary and moved to Boulder, Colorado, where she used her own money to kick-start the new organization.

"There are a lot of rabbis who are good at congregational work," Korngold says. "But few are good [at] using the environment as a tool, at connecting with the kind of population that isn't interested in congregations. I happen to be one of them."

When Korngold can't officiate herself, she outsources the responsibility of the life-cycle event to someone within a professional network of other rabbis or even rabbinical students who might be available instead. Adventure Rabbi has attracted a sizable number of participants who've taken advantage of its services. Yet while this allows a greater number of people to experience Jewish ritual in the great outdoors, I think it also raises some problems. This "farming out" system transforms spiritual teachers and guides into interchangeable functionaries, and it does nothing to foster any sort of ongoing relationship between rabbi and participant. Korngold is aware of this issue and is seeking ways of addressing it.

Despite the many shortcomings of congregational Judaism, do we really want to create a rent-a-rabbi situation where a person can essentially blow off any meaningful connection to the larger Jewish community and treat sacred ritual and the rabbinic relationship in a private, goods-for-services kind of way? I have the same problem with parents who choose to observe their child's bar or bat mitzvah ceremony in Israel, far away from home and relatives, and with young Jewish couples who hold destination weddings in lovely but remote venues.

Is a rabbi just a prop for our personal desires, a hired gun used to satisfy our need to be different and cool?

Where's our fidelity to the classic idea that most Jewish life-cycle rituals are meant to be *public* events, ones to be shared with and celebrated by the community as a whole, including not only family members but complete strangers? To put it in starker, less philosophical terms, how is eighty-seven-year-old Aunt Miriam going to make it down to Costa Rica, or up Mount Hood, for her beloved great-niece's wedding—to be given the gift, as the Jewish marriage blessing states, of "rejoicing with bride and groom"?

Are we, despite our best intentions, only the products of our narcissistic culture? When it comes down to it, is everything ultimately about *me me me*?

Religious education is one thing. As far as I'm concerned it can and should take place anywhere and everywhere it works:

You can learn about Judaism from a book or from a moun-
taintop. But religious life-cycle ceremonies—Jewish rites of
passage—are something else, and all of us in this very new
field need to be cautious about how we proceed. While the former is about individual literacy, the latter is ultimately about
community, about linking generations of Jews across the mystical spectrum of history and geography, from the wilderness
of Sinai to the valley of Silicon.

Like mainstream Judaism, extreme Judaism has its own
share of flaws. When the boundary between religion's public
and private spheres isn't handled with care, the line between
selflessness and selfishness, humility and hubris, becomes
blurry. How in the world do I, as a Jewish teacher, impart basic Jewish values like commitment (to be there for others) and
interdependence (within a communal context) if I'm off free-
lancing with a family in some desert setting, reciting a liturgy
of gratitude and announcing the Hebrew name of a newborn
baby—not to the assembled household of Israel, but to a gathering of sagebrush and scorpions?

That's not gonzo; that's just bizarre. While God may be
everywhere, organized religion is a human construct. We
might be able to commune with the divine in any place and
through any experience, but the special rites we perform that
are meant to affirm and celebrate God's reality and presence in
our lives reach their highest level only in association with *other*
humans.

Another well-intentioned but problematic trend within the
movement for a more nature-based, adrenaline-juiced Judaism is its awkward attempt to sometimes interweave Native
American practices with Jewish ones. In some ways this is a
logical if misguided consequence of our context. Native
American rituals, ceremonies, and spirituality somehow ring

more authentic and true to Westernized, disaffected Americans who feel far removed from the roots of their respective faiths and who are searching for something more soulful in their native soil. We find this phenomenon in the men's movement, the women's movement, and in segments of Christianity and Judaism.

I'd bet a thousand bucks more Jews have heard of Black Elk than Bezalel (the biblical artisan who designed the Tabernacle in the wilderness).

We need to be wary. I know firsthand the power of sweat lodges and vision quests. But it is one thing to be a respectful observer of other traditions, and another to be an active participant in them. C'mon, Jews are no more Sioux than Muslims are Mohican, and any forced, false attempt to meld our different and frequently divergent sacred systems of belief and behavior erodes the integrity of each of them. In our zeal to reinfuse Judaism with the elemental and experiential spirituality it so often seems to lack, we risk falling into the pit of syncretism—of trying to combine, in artificial ways, doctrines and rites of passage that are entirely incompatible. The good news is that we don't need to look elsewhere. Judaism has powerful practices, too. That's part of what I want to reveal and recover through this book.

Let's just suck it up, pick one spiritual heritage, and stick to it.

But sometimes spirituality and religion are the last things on the minds of the organizers of and participants in Jewish outdoor adventures. Several of today's groups are more interested in simply bringing Jews together for exciting social or cultural events in beautiful, natural settings. Often, of course, shared experience and positive bonding with other Jews leads to a renewed commitment to the Jewish community in general, as well as to a heightened sense of personal Jewish identity.

Mosaic Outdoor Clubs of America is an example of one of these groups. More a loose network of chapters than a formal, centralized organization, Mosaic has over twenty-five individual clubs throughout the United States, Canada, and Israel. It began in 1988 with only a single chapter, when Steve Millmond organized a hike in the Colorado Rockies with other local, marginally connected Jews. Mosaic—named for Moses, whom the network's Web site refers to as the original "outdoor Jew"—now offers a wide range of activities to Jews of all ages, both married and single, who share a love of the outdoors and nature. Every Labor Day weekend the different clubs gather for an Annual Mosaic International Event. Past events have taken place in Colorado, Vermont, Georgia, North Carolina, and elsewhere.

Millmond formed Mosaic because he felt that modern Jews had lost touch with the fact that historical Jewish life was intimately linked with the environment. Since, in his view, so many of today's Jews would rather be "dining out and shopping" rather than camping and canoeing, those who did desire the excitement of outdoor activity were forced to join up with largely non-Jewish groups in order to satisfy their craving. This led to more intermarriage and a deeper disconnect with the Jewish community. Millmond wanted to bring together Jews who had an interest in nature as well as those who didn't, but who might get hooked as a result of a trip.

Nearly two decades later, not only have Mosaic members married one another, but the network has branched out and begun to engage in leadership training and social action projects (such as trail cleanups).

Travel Jewish offers yet another model of a nonreligious organization that seeks to blend stimulating, mostly outdoor travel with Jewish community and identity. Deb Miller, an avid and lifelong traveler, created Travel Jewish in 2000 with a single question that she took as a personal, then as a professional, challenge: Since so many Jews like to travel, and since so few like synagogues, how do we connect Jewish travelers with local Jewish communities and cultures in noncongregational contexts? At the time Miller was married to an Argentinean Jew and living in Buenos Aires. The Israeli embassy there had been bombed by terrorists in 1992, and the Argentine Israelite Mutual Aid Association (known by its Spanish acronym, AMIA) had been blown up in 1994, leaving almost a hundred dead. Jewish issues were very much at the forefront of Miller's mind during her three years in that capital.

At first Miller simply arranged day tours of "Jewish Argentina" for Jewish tourists who were already there. The outings—which matched Jewish travelers with Jewish locals and their histories—were such a success that Miller decided, after she returned to the United States and with her contacts in place, to offer more extended trips that focused on Jewish life and culture in South America. In addition to Argentina, Travel Jewish has run trips to Brazil, Chile, and Uruguay. Participants have tasted kosher Chilean wine in private homes and accompanied fellow Jews to their places of work, to art galleries, and to tango halls. Miller also offers specialized trips for singles and women, as well as eco-tours into Patagonia and the Pantanal. One day she hopes to organize trips to other parts of the world to, in her words, "bring the global Jewish community together."

Most of those who have joined one of Travel Jewish's cultural and identity adventures have had profound experiences that have ignited (or reignited) an interest in Jewish communal life. Yet Miller often feels alone and unheard. Her challenge, like that of nearly everyone else in this chapter, is simply getting the word out. Without wider support, very few of us

will ever hear Ladino spoken over a picnic lunch, or ride
horses in the shadow of Jewish gauchos.

As different from one another as many of these adventure
groups are, one quality they share is a willingness to fail. Yet
by boldly reaching into new frontiers for Jewish expression, by
being willing to take risks, they are meeting people where they
are and reaching hundreds, perhaps thousands, of detached,
alienated Jews—even if that means traveling far away from a
synagogue or deep into a challenging wilderness environment
to inspire them. All of these organizations strive, each in their
own unique way, to bring Judaism to Jews and Jews back to
Judaism.

In an era when free time is at a premium, extreme approaches to faith combine activities that many Jews like to do already with a religious and ethical framework that might seem
irrelevant to them in more conventional contexts. These programs *work,* and Jewish leaders are shortsighted dodos for not
doing more to help them succeed on a national scale, by making them more accessible and visible. But these journeys will
take us only so far. If we learn to focus on the needs of others,
though, as well as on our own, outdoor adventures can serve as
wonderful vehicles to aid in the growth of a more vivacious
and dynamic Jewish community.

But what if you can't afford one of these trips? And what if
you just can't find one of these groups in your city or town?

Nothing should hold you back. Take the initiative and create your own extreme religious event.

Call some friends and travel to a scenic location or a national park. If you're planning a day trip, pack a lunch. If you
want your experience to last a few days or more, pack a tent.
Ask a local rabbi for Jewish texts that relate to the themes of
the experience you have in mind, texts on teamwork, facing

challenges, gaining perspective, the environment. *You* decide what you'd like to explore from your spiritual tradition. Or ask that rabbi to help organize a trip through his or her synagogue. If you're on your own, hire a professional guide to handle the adventure component of your excursion, whether it involves rock climbing, kayaking, or caving. And if your outdoor adventure runs over a weekend, why not incorporate a ritual aspect into it by bringing candles, wine, and a challah so you can celebrate Shabbat?

Don't wait around for someone to bring this kind of experience to you—go to it. You have more control over your Jewish life than you think.

Nature and Judaism are on the same page when it comes to showing us our true place in the cosmos. Citing the order of Creation in the first chapter of the book of Genesis, the Talmud asks, "Why were human beings created last?" That seems a very reasonable question, since so many of us, especially today, think of ourselves (and, when we have them, our children) as God's gifts to the universe. The Talmud itself provides the answer: "So that [humanity] should never grow proud and arrogant—for one can reply to them, 'Even the gnat came before you in Creation!'"

Bearing witness to an ominous, fifty-thousand-foot thunderhead, or to the otherworldly pulsations of the Northern Lights, or to the dense impenetrability of the Amazon rainforests can have a similar effect on us. Embedded in both nature and Jewish theology is the same existential message: *We ain't all that.* It's a message that most of us don't really want to hear. Yet the religious perspective is, fundamentally, a perspective of extreme, radical humility. More than a wake-up call, it's a shake-up call: Whether we like it or not, we're connected to something much bigger than ourselves.

Deal with it.

That's why Judaism, when presented in its best and most authentic light, doesn't coddle—it confronts. I wouldn't have it, or transmit it, any other way. Who wants to be part of some lame-ass religion that treats us with kid gloves? By challenging us to see the world and ourselves in new ways, by taking us out of our comfort zones and placing us squarely into contexts that are sometimes unfamiliar and unsettling—hell, that's how we evolve and mature. With self-awareness comes self-affirmation, and a stronger and deeper appreciation of life.

Judaism isn't about making us feel good or numbing our discomfort; it isn't, as Marx argued about religion in general, an opiate. Go buy a dime bag or a bottle of absinthe if that's all you're after.

Judaism is about forcing us to be real.

But is this what we're seeing out there in the "real" Jewish world? Most of the time, no. It's either facile and false, or dull to the point of paralysis. That's why what we need now, what we need desperately, is both a rejection *and* a return. We must learn to embrace paradox. We should question authority and challenge the status quo, but we've got to do it through the excavation of traditional—yet often radical and sometimes subversive—teachings that have been warped or whitewashed over time, if we are to have credibility and perspective.

We need to look back in order to move ahead. We've got to reclaim our rebel roots.

CHAPTER 3

Out with the New,
In with the Old

THE EARLY SAGES STATED: "He who has never witnessed the Celebration of the Drawing of the Waters has never experienced true joy in his life." This ancient, mysterious, barely known rite—which was once a vital part of the annual fall pilgrimage to Jerusalem during the sacred festival of Sukkot—was very nearly lost to the ages after the destruction of the Second Temple two thousand years ago. If the rabbis were right, what are the implications for Jews and Jewish observance today? Will we ever reach the level of joy and exuberance that our forebears did?

We don't know what we're missing.

Literally.

Yet Gen Xers and Gen Yers, including those who are interested and active in Jewish life, are always searching for the next new thing—whatever's the most popular, trendiest, hippest game in town. If the Internet is hot, they look for ways of fusing it with Judaism. If corporate branding is the rage, they try to market their institutions, programs, and frequently themselves with that strategy in mind.

Too many of these new models, if they're not downright forced and stupid, demonstrate an inexcusable lack of imagination, and a number of the old ones are actually strikingly profound—all we need to do is tweak them and make them more relevant to our times. And the great thing about these ancient, lost practices is that they're right under our Jewish schnozolas, if we'd only sniff around a little while.

That's why there's a small movement afoot to excavate, recover, and reclaim many previously unknown or disregarded rituals. Ironically, these old practices are being revived by some of the Jewish community's youngest members.

Now back to the water-drawing celebration, or, in Hebrew, *Simchat Beit ha-Shoevah.* The weeklong holiday of Sukkot, originally an autumn harvest festival in the land of Israel, has been observed in modern times in lovely but fairly straightforward ways: Jews go to synagogue for special worship services; parents and children build and decorate outdoor *sukkot,* or huts, in which they sometimes eat meals or sleep; and the *lulav* and *etrog,* organic, fragrant ritual objects, are shaken in the various directions of the universe. While our Sukkot liturgy contains a few brief prayers for rain and a good harvest, that residue is all that hints at the festival's mystical, murky roots.

In the Temple era, Sukkot was referred to as *he-Chag,* or "*the* Holiday"—it was considered more important to the spiritual and communal life of the Jewish people than even Rosh Hashanah and Yom Kippur. Why? There were other pilgrimage festivals, other opportunities for prayer and sacrifice. What made Sukkot qualitatively different from all of the other holy days was the beauty, mystery, and joyful intensity of the Celebration of the Drawing of the Waters.

Which raises the question: Where have all the waters gone?

In the fall of 2000, The New Shul, in collaboration with Amichai Lau-Lavie, founder and director of Storahtelling (a brash and innovative group I'll highlight later in the chapter), held our community's first full-blown Jewish Rain Dance, a modern—or, more accurately, *post*modern—interpretation of Sukkot's ancient water-drawing rite. Our observance of that rite has evolved ever since, with great popularity and success. Yet other than Storahtelling's continuing, roving productions of it, only a handful of synagogues that I am aware of, besides ours, have attempted to revive this primal and powerful expression of Jewish spirituality that most Jews don't even know exists.

There is a passage hidden deep within the tomes of the Talmud that describes briefly, but in detail, the elaborate ceremony of *Simchat Beit ha-Shoevah*. It is a fifteen-hundred-year-old description of an event that took place many centuries before that, and it reads like the screenplay for *Raiders of the Lost Ark*—emotionally and visually arresting, a bit over the top, yet ultimately fulfilling and transporting.

In one of the holiest sections of the Temple complex, and to the synchronized accompaniment of musical instruments, Levites and priests (wearing their special ceremonial garb) would perform the rite. As the Levites chanted the fifteen Psalms of Ascent (Psalms 120–34), the priests would congregate and ascend—bowls of holy water cupped in their hands—one step for each psalm, until they reached the top of an elevated platform. From there, the individual bowls would be poured into a single, large urn, and the water libation—and ceremony as a whole—would be complete. The Celebration of the Drawing of the Waters ended with the rapturous words of Psalm 135: "Hallelujah! Praise the name of God! Give praise, you servants of God!"

That's all we know about a glorious Jewish ritual that nearly vanished from our collective memory. Yet it is a ritual that warrants new exposure and renewed life. Some of us have been working toward achieving those goals.

Today, the ram's horn (or *shofar*) is used almost exclusively during the Days of Awe, to serve, as the great rabbi-philosopher Moses Maimonides claimed in the twelfth century, as a vehicle "to wake us from our moral slumber." In its historical context, however, the *shofar* served many purposes. One of them was as a call for the Israelites to assemble— for sacred observance, for a national census, or, when necessary, for war. It's a shame, and a missed opportunity, that the *shofar* is utilized so rarely in the modern era and in Jewish communal life, since the spiraled ram's horn is, to me, the most riveting and hauntingly beautiful ritual instrument in Judaism.

My community's observance of *Simchat Beit ha-Shoevah* always begins with a single, long blast from the *shofar*. It is our call to gather for the start of the celebration, an event where the ancient Near East meets a sort of religious Cirque du Soleil.

The creation of the right atmosphere and environment is everything. The aim of religious ritual is, or ought to be, connecting with and inspiring our hearts, souls, and heads. It should transport and transform us. When the ram's horn is sounded and people walk into our main hall, we try to make them feel as if they've entered another world. As with our observance of Purim, the room is lit and decorated as befits the theme of the holiday. For the Sukkot water-drawing celebration, the lights are dim and mystical; exotic music is being performed. The walls are draped with Middle Eastern–style fabrics. Many of the men and women—our urban Levites and priests—are dressed in white. Instead of a Persian palace, our hall has been changed into the courtyards and altars of the holy Temple in Jerusalem.

A large pool filled with water sits conspicuously in the center of the room.

Ours is a reinterpretation, not a re-creation, of *Simchat Beit ha-Shoevah*. In an effort to make the ritual more relevant to our time and place, we have eliminated some elements and added others. Though reenactment is a feature of our event, what we are after is not its historicity, but its spirituality. We want to recover Judaism's lost power, not its obsolete institutions. Using that as a guide, our celebration interweaves core aspects of the original ceremony—such as the recitation of the Psalms of Ascent and the drawing and pouring of water—with a dramatized retelling, incorporating hypnotic, ravelike drumming and dance, of a related story about King David. In this story the young leader accidentally unleashes the dormant primordial waters of chaos and nearly destroys the world. It is only after the fifteen psalms are chanted that the waters return to a level that allows them to nourish, rather than overwhelm, the earth and its inhabitants.

By the end, everyone in the room gets it. An archaic and arcane rite that was originally designed to petition God for rain has been retooled into a contemporary, stirring celebration—not only of God's grace, but of life itself.

Why is an unknown, somewhat strange rite like the Jewish Rain Dance so effective among those few groups and congregations that observe it? Why does Cirque du Soleil have four sold-out shows running simultaneously on Las Vegas's Strip every night? It's because of their festive, mysterious, multisensory, interactive, and intergenerational natures. Parents and children can find their own unique places within the many and varied elements (action, music, dance, song, narrative) in the event's structure. And like an ecstatic experience at a rave concert, even young Jews—that most elusive of our demographic populations—find themselves moved in their bodies and souls, often for the very first time, by organized religion.

Marvel of marvels, there's something for everyone. Something much deeper than mere entertainment.

Here's what's bizarre: If this ceremony works so well, then why don't more communities observe it? Part of it is ignorance. Most of us, including rabbis, simply don't know about *Simchat Beit ha-Shoevah* (and other esoteric but still meaningful rituals and rites). Even if more of us did, we certainly aren't all equipped to mount a full-fledged, dynamic presentation of it. So exposure and education—or rather excavation and reclamation—have to be among our top priorities. We must observe and learn from others. Had The New Shul not forged an initial partnership with Storahtelling, a group that already had some experience with this recovered celebration, the event would never have taken root in our community.

We have to take risks and experiment. We have to stay humble.

And we must be willing to fail.

Yet many Jewish religious leaders are opposed in principle to the act of excavating ancient practices. For them, these beautiful rituals are not lost, but no longer relevant, at least in the theological sense. Traditionalist colleagues of mine claim that the water-drawing celebration can't be performed without a "real" Temple and a "real" priesthood. My more progressive colleagues aren't bothered by that point. But they argue that if it is acceptable to bring back *some* practices from the Temple period, why not bring back *all* of them? In other words, if it's okay for us to offer ceremonial water libations, what's to stop the reinstatement of the biblical caste system, or the reintroduction of animal sacrifice?

This is chimp logic.

Ralph Waldo Emerson wrote that consistency is the hobgoblin of small minds. Who cares if we're inconsistent? All we need to do is use a little common sense. What the hell is wrong with breathing fresh air into some resurfaced practices while keeping others dead and buried? Tedium is the stepchild of consistency, and tedium is precisely what too many Jews experience when they walk into a synagogue today. My reaction to the traditionalist argument is equally pragmatic: Should we trash Judaism's unearthed jewels just because they don't sit comfortably within the framework of Jewish doctrine? No. We should, instead, tap into the power of our imaginations, of our capacity to treat ritual as metaphor rather than as artifact. That's why, during the Passover Seder, we say that we, too, were slaves in the land of Egypt— not because we're role-playing, but because, in a mythic way, we're *reliving*.

I want more tradition, not less. More enchantment, less routine.

But what if you don't want to go to a synagogue or a communal event in order to experience that sense of enchantment? Though there are some great models out there in our cities and suburbs, they're not for everybody.

The gonzo Jew often has an ambivalent relationship with institutional Judaism. That's not a problem—it's an opportunity. While some of the little-known, previously discarded rites and celebrations that some of us have begun to resurrect and refashion trace their origins to Temple times (such as *Simchat Beit ha-Shoevah*), others are drawn from more recent mystical traditions, where the focus is more frequently on the individual and the private home than on the community as a whole.

The key to becoming a spiritual archaeologist is having a bold and open mind, and being receptive to ritual's mystery and power. If we do that, then, like Indiana Jones, we can turn our personal quest for meaning into the most exciting of adventures.

If synagogues aren't for you, or you can't push your congregation's leadership to experiment with compelling new/old rituals, then what can you do—especially around the holidays—to enhance and elevate your spiritual life as a Jew? In Chapter 1, we looked at two Hasidic spiritual practices, the *tish* and *hitbodedut,* and at how they are being revamped and played out in some of today's communities. Hasidism has a lot to say in the area of private, home observance as well. If the goal of mainstream religion is to serve God (through worship, ritual and ethical practice, and study), then the goal of mystical Judaism, to which Hasidism belongs, is to *experience* God.

And you don't need a pew or a pulpit for that to happen.

What a lot of people don't realize about the highly individualistic New Age movement is that for all its popular appeal among contemporary seekers, many of its practices and insights aren't new at all. They're drawn from the "antiquated" world of organized religion it so often puts down. Let's take the Jewish Sabbath, for instance. Most American Jews don't observe it, find it meaningful, or care about it in the slightest. Yet some of those very same Jews flock to New Age meditation and healing centers by the hordes—in search of the spirituality and serenity that Shabbat is *designed* to instill in us. The problem isn't with Shabbat, but with the fact that most of us aren't aware of some of the most beautiful and transporting practices associated with it.

To start with one example, incense is big these days. (It was a pretty hot spiritual item in the Temple era thousands of years ago, but that's another story.) Hasidism, as a mystical movement that grasped that our senses have as much power as our brains in unlocking the doors to transcendence, has a great deal to say about *preparation* for observance—about setting the right mood. Most of us know that you can't really have an intense and successful weight-training or cardio workout without getting your body ready beforehand with some serious stretching exercises. And you don't get the most out of the Shabbat experience without putting in similar prep work on your soul. The use of incense has proven to be an effective spiritual warm-up technique for a long time, particularly in mystical circles.

Many of the original Hasidim, in the eighteenth and nineteenth centuries, would light incense, or occasionally set out dishes of fragrant spices, prior to sunset on Friday afternoon. The distinctive and pleasant scent would suggest to them the special and joyous character of the Sabbath that would soon pervade their homes—just like the pleasing odor that was permeating their rooms.

Aside from engendering this feeling of heightened anticipation, scent was also viewed as a means of expanding spiritual consciousness. The Talmud itself asks, "What is it that the soul enjoys yet does nothing for the body?" Its answer: "A pleasant scent." Shabbat is supposed to be a purely *meta*physical experience. What better way to prepare for it than with a tool intended to touch the spirit alone?

Scientists have done studies on the power of olfaction, and it is clear that scent is one of the most intense and immediate of the human senses: A single odor can trigger memories, emotions, and experiences in an instant. It can take us away to distant and dreamlike places. At times, some Hasidic masters (including the movement's founder, the Baal Shem Tov) even used snuff to concentrate their minds and help carry them to supernal realms during prayer and study. One of them went so far as to claim that his own snuffbox contained nothing less than the sweet aroma of the Garden of Eden itself—it could be smelled, however, only with the advent of Shabbat, and only by a person who was receptive to it.

Though most of us don't use snuff today, try to use incense or a spice box to create a more meaningful and personalized Shabbat. You don't need a synagogue to welcome the Sabbath Bride. Just imagine the sweet fragrance of the Garden of Eden and see where your soul transports you.

Another spiritual exercise to use to prepare for and enhance Shabbat, and that can be practiced at home, involves light, that most primal and mythic of elements. Many Jews know that Shabbat officially begins when we light two candles, usually on our dinner table, and recite the *kiddush* blessing over a cup of wine. But there are other mystical traditions that are virtually unheard of and rarely observed, just waiting to be rediscovered by a new generation. There is, for instance, the simple Hasidic custom of lighting, before the onset of Shabbat, a large number of nonceremonial candles in the room where you will eat your festive meal, as well as at least one in each other room of your home. What is the idea behind the practice? Increased light paves the way for, and mirrors, the increased spiritual light of Shabbat.

The mystics had a numerological field day with candle configurations. Some followed the custom of lighting seven candles for the seven days of the week; others lit ten, to represent the Ten Commandments. One intriguing pre-Hasidic custom involved lighting exactly thirty-six candles, symbolizing the thirty-six hours that the biblical Adam had the benefit of the divine light before it was hidden away after his expulsion from Eden. Where did that particular number originate? Adam was created on the sixth day, the day before Shabbat.

On that day he had use of this light for twelve hours. Combined with the twenty-four hours of light that followed on the seventh day—since the Sabbath, even when it is dark, is a time of unadulterated, sacred light—Adam bathed in divine luminosity for thirty-six hours. Seen in this way, Shabbat is Eden all over again, our weekly taste of primeval bliss.

So construct your own special symbolism. Come up with numbers that have meaning for you and relevance to your life. Imitate God at the moment of Creation. Let there be light! Let the light of enchantment illuminate your house or apartment.

We can create amazing new practices by learning from old ones. But as important as they are, don't focus excessively on atmosphere and decor. Try to alter your mind-set, too. Follow the pathway of the mystics and open the portal of your imagination.

There's some great stuff in need of retrieval.

Why not give it a shot before you shoot it down?

Storahtelling: Jewish Ritual Theater Revived is a contemporary group of young Jewish educators, musicians, and performance artists devoted to, among other interests, the retrieval and reclamation of unobserved or forgotten Jewish practices and celebrations—particularly those related to the public reading of the Torah. Storahtelling was conceived and founded in New York City in 1998 by Israeli-born Amichai Lau-Lavie while he was working as an educator at Congregation B'nai Jeshurun on Manhattan's Upper West Side.

Lau-Lavie's journey is itself a story of rejection, retrieval, and revival. Brought up and educated in the tradition-entrenched Orthodox Israeli yeshiva world (and having an uncle who served as the country's chief rabbi for Ashkenazi Jews), Lau-Lavie's life was suffused with, but eventually

oppressed by, a rigid kind of Judaism he felt forced to abandon. With a rich and strong background in Judaic learning
embedded within him, Lau-Lavie traveled to the more plural-
istic shores of the United States soon after he finished his military service.

Determined to breathe new life into a central rite of Jewish
worship and, historically, of Jewish life, Storahtelling interweaves the weekly Torah portion with stories, dramatization,
music, humor, and communal participation.

Lau-Lavie feels that the vast majority of Torah services in
synagogues are staid, stuffy, and achingly unexciting affairs.
To him, that represents a break with Jewish tradition, not a
continuation of it. For centuries, Lau-Lavie argues, the purpose of the Torah reading "was to engage the entire community in a storytelling event that nourishes the community with
meaning and relevance." That's why, in the past, the Torah
would sometimes be read near the marketplace or in the public square. The ritual was brought to the people, not the other
way around.

"Many of my peers don't go to synagogue because they're
bored to death," says Lau-Lavie. "But they do go to movies and
the theater, and that's where their souls are tapped." It is a primary goal of Storahtelling to utilize, unabashedly, some of
those same dramatic and theatrical elements in order to create a
more powerful emotional and spiritual experience in the context of religion—as well as one that is more popular and in tune
with pop culture.

"We offer a way," Lau-Lavie says, "to tap into the tradition,
into ourselves, into the narratives of our community in a manner that is captivating and fresh and deeply engaging. When
people go to the theater, they're wearing their entertainment
hat, their hearts are open, and expectations are high. That
brings out a certain type of behavior. When people go to syna-

gogue, they don't have the same emotional agenda. We want to make people at synagogue as excited about that as they are at the theater."

In important ways, what Storahtelling provides isn't an avant-garde approach to Judaism but a return to a lost tradition. Jews once allowed their religious rituals and sacred texts to incorporate theatricality with much more comfort. One way in which that lost theatrical tradition has been reintroduced and reshaped by Storahtelling is through its use of a *meturgemon,* or "interpretive translator."

After researching early post-Temple Torah services, Lau-Lavie discovered that up until about one thousand years ago, Torah readings were frequently accompanied by a *meturgemon,* a member of the community who could translate the original Hebrew verses (which only the most educated classes could follow) into the vernacular of the time and place. That person would also offer a running commentary, or *midrash,* to the assembly before him. When the Torah service grew longer and the rabbinic sermon was added, the *meturgemon* disappeared from the Jewish scene.

"It was live subtitles," says Lau-Lavie. "He would translate the text, but also highlight the subtext and context of what the story was about. So he was both a storyteller and a living bridge between the past and the present. I was amazed at how little was known about this ritual and its history."

Storahtelling has revived and reclaimed this forgotten practice and beefed it up with modern—and controversial—techniques. When a synagogue enlists Storahtelling to participate in one of its services, the rabbi or cantor will typically chant a verse or two from the Torah scroll and then pause. Storahtelling performers will then dramatize the passage in English, often in costume and to the accompaniment of live music. Says the group's founder: "We are taking an ancient form of sacred storytelling, with clear guidelines and instructions, that's been in the attic for a thousand years, and we are adding a contemporary form somewhere between story and theater. I can argue with any rabbi who says this isn't kosher until I'm blue in the face, and I'll be right."

Like a *meturgemon* of old, Storahtelling always strives for relevance—though sometimes it comes at the expense of reverence. Some in the Jewish community think Storahtelling has crossed the line into pandering and shtick.

"We're not doing this for the rabbis or people who are scholarly and know the story well," Lau-Lavie says. "We're doing this for the people who don't, which is the majority. Whenever anyone sees this and says it's too cute, it's too funny, it's not deep enough, I say that it may seem that way to you because you know it. For most people, this is their first taste of Torah as something relevant, and if they want more they can follow up and they can read more. This is an invitation."

There is another significant way in which the ritual performers of this traveling troupe, as well as some of the adventure rabbis from the preceding chapter, have, perhaps unwittingly, resurrected an ancient, little-known model and made it meaningful to our own era and zeitgeist.

Some of the earliest sages, from nearly two thousand years ago, are depicted in Jewish legends and literature as wandering teachers, spiritual zealots willing to go far and wide in order to spread the wisdom of their faith. The *maggid*—the itinerant Jewish teacher and preacher—was part of a kind of nonestablishment intelligentsia, and was especially active by the late Middle Ages and beyond. Detached from or only loosely connected to permanent congregations, the *maggid* would, out of personal zeal and/or professional need, roam the countryside to instruct and inspire largely uneducated, illiter-

ate Jews who were then living on the geographical and socio-
logical periphery of the Jewish world.

As modern-day itinerants, Storahtellers and adventure
rabbis are also trying to reach those on the margins of Jewish
life, what today we Jewish professionals call "the unaffiliated."
These men and women—many, but certainly not all of them,
under forty—feel little or no attachment to Judaism or its institutions and practices. They are a talented but terribly underserved population, and their Jewish literacy is minimal or
nonexistent. Yet they are on our radar screens because they are
hungry for spiritual sustenance, moral guidance, and a sense
of community. Still, we can't wait for them to come to us. We
have to reach out to them.

So some of us hit the road. Unlike our forebears, though,
our target destinations aren't the remote farms and shtetls of
Eastern Europe.

They are theater spaces, nightclubs, and national parks.

For the young, hip, contemporary Jews who venture into such
places, the concept of making a pilgrimage, in its historic and
religious sense, probably seems as antiquated and alien as a
slide rule. Yet people today make these kinds of pilgrimages
every year, as their parents and grandparents did before them:
Muslims travel to Mecca, Catholics to Rome, Hindus to the
Ganges. These physical and sometimes challenging journeys
are powerful rites that connect modern people with their past,
with their spiritual and cultural identities, and with each
other.

Judaism shares this ancient pilgrimage tradition, though it
has lost much of its obvious relevance—and its meaning—
since the Second Temple was destroyed. Our faith once
involved three great, annual pilgrimage events to the Holy
Land and its sacred capital of Jerusalem: Sukkot (the Feast of

Tabernacles), Passover (the Feast of Unleavened Bread), and Shavuot (the Feast of Weeks). Jewish men, women, and children would travel to the Temple from the many and varied Diaspora communities in order to offer sacrifices and prayers.

Even after the Temple was gone and the Holy Land was occupied by a long list of foreign powers (e.g., Romans, Crusaders, Ottomans), Jews would, over the centuries and often at enormous personal risk, make private pilgrimages to sacred sites. Some would sneak into Jerusalem to glimpse the Western Wall, all that was left of the once glorious Temple complex. Some would journey south to Hebron, to the Cave of the Patriarchs and Matriarchs. Others would travel north to the Galilee to pay homage at the graves of Kabbalists such as Rabbi Isaac Luria and other luminaries.

For the pilgrim, these experiences were intense and intimate.

They were also mythic, mystical, and frequently life altering.

But much of that power remained untapped—until recently. For a very, very long time, Israel had morphed into a metaphor. Except for the fortunate few who were able to taste of the Land of Milk and Honey directly, Jerusalem (along with the other gems of the Holy Land) was not a tactile place but an ethereal object of Jewish imagination and aspiration, the spiritual symbol toward which our people turned their planted bodies three times a day in prayer. Whatever pilgrimages *did* occur were primarily ones that played out in our ancestors' minds, hearts, and souls.

Things changed dramatically on May 14, 1948, with the establishment of the modern state of Israel.

Now, in the wake of that historic, monumental event, ours is the first generation in two millennia to live in a world where a vibrant, flesh-and-blood Jewish nation is a solid, tangible, given fact.

That's because for the generation of Jews before us, Israel hadn't yet been fully liberated from the level of metaphor. In a post-Holocaust world where the scars were still fresh and raw, a Jewish state—populated by builders and farmers and soldiers—became a symbol of survival and a source of pride. It was the beacon of light that followed the abyss of darkness. Some Jews moved there and became citizens of the young state; others traveled to visit; most, however, stayed home and wrote checks to Jewish organizations in support of their spiritual and cultural homeland.

For us, the new generation, Israel is a grounded, political entity. Since it is no longer just a metaphor, but a country whose decisions affect those around them, the rules have changed. You can't disagree with a symbol, but you can question the policies of a government. That is a sign of strength and maturity. What you can't question is the power—once it is tapped—of the relationship between Jews in the Diaspora and in the Jewish homeland. While that relationship, like all authentic relationships, is a fluid one, it is, for many of us, the sole basis of our identities as Jews.

Our relationship with Israel—not the rituals of the Jewish religion—is frequently what makes Jewishness relevant and meaningful.

Whether we Jewish leaders like this phenomenon or not (and I'll discuss some of its problems later), it is as much a fact of our communal life as is Israel itself. A relationship with the Jewish state, however, can cultivate and catalyze a relationship with Judaism. But you can't bring Israel to Jews—you need to bring Jews to Israel. Nothing will happen unless Jewish feet walk on Jewish soil.

We must renew the rite of pilgrimage for the contemporary Jew.

It has started to happen. In 1999, as a result of a partnership among Jewish philanthropists, organizations, foundations, and the government of Israel itself, Birthright Israel was created. Its stated mission was very clear and very simple, but colossal in its scope and ambition: It is the birthright of every Jew, especially as they begin to explore and develop their individual identities, to receive a free trip to Israel as a *gift* from the Jewish community. The only requirement is desire. Any Jew between the ages of eighteen and twenty-six who has never been to Israel before is entitled to one of these ten-day trips. To date, approximately one hundred thousand young adults from forty countries have traveled—or made pilgrimages—to Israel through the Birthright program.

What the original partners of Birthright recognized was the ability of an Israel experience, even one that lasted only ten days, to transform young Jewish lives. These trips have ignited intense cultural and spiritual identification and emotion in thousands of previously disinterested Jews, diminished the division between Israel and Diaspora communities around the world, promoted the role of Israel as a vital resource for Jewish history, identity, and learning, and increased the number of return visits participants make to the Jewish state.

Like the pilgrimages of prior eras, these trips also have a mythic quality to them, if you dig deeply enough.

Whether it is conscious behavior or not, each Birthright "pilgrim" is walking in the footsteps of his or her forebears, crossing the same rivers, climbing the same sandy hills, bearing witness to the same holy sites. Nearly everything at the heart of the biblical history of the Jewish people is linked to the land of Israel: Jerusalem, the religious and political center, city of David and Solomon; the Negev desert and Beersheba, where Isaac found water for his flocks and family; the Galilee and Mount Carmel, where the prophet Elijah confronted idolaters; the Jordan River, Joshua's gateway to the Promised Land.

You open the Bible and read a passage about a particular place, and there it is, right in front of you. You can walk over it, touch it, even swim in it. The events that occurred there may have happened long ago, but their ghostly memories are still alive.

In Israel, time and space collapse.

Like the obscure rituals and practices we looked at earlier in this chapter, Israel itself—depending on our attitudes and receptivity—can be both old and new simultaneously. To make a journey there, to convene en masse with other Jews from around the world on the same soil that so many past generations have visited, is to recover and reclaim the ancient rite of pilgrimage. There is great power in this primal, epic act. Even a brief trip to Israel can become an existential slap in our face, a wake-up call to experience the sights and sounds that have made us who we are.

What do you do if you don't qualify for a free Birthright trip? What if you're a Jew over twenty-six who has never been to Israel before? Suck it up, move your butt, and find your own path to the Promised Land. If money is an issue, do a little research and be creative. Contact a local federation group (discussed later in the book) or synagogue—they almost always offer subsidized "missions" to Israel that you can hook up with. Or join a volunteer program: work on a kibbutz or at an absorption center for new immigrants. Don't view your visit to Israel as a political endorsement of that country's governmental policies, but as an imaginative enactment of a mythic (even mystical) reunion with Jewish brothers and sisters you've never met, with ancestral soil you've never stood on.

What on the surface might appear to us as cutting edge, experimental, or avant-garde can be, in reality, as traditional as the Torah itself. That's why efforts to rediscover and revitalize Judaism's lost practices are so important to our own era. We need anchors of identity and spirituality, strong anchors with long ropes that keep us from drifting away, not heavy and cumbersome ones that immobilize us or threaten to drag us down. The gonzo approach to religious life runs fiercely *counter* to much of today's cultural perspective on the subject. It rejects a world of black-and-white alternatives, the false dichotomy—and false choice—between an inflexible literalism or a rigid secularism.

But gonzo isn't about limp-wristed moderation. It's about the fearless embrace of murky and extreme ambiguity.

Jesse Ventura, former professional wrestler and governor of Minnesota, once claimed proudly to the press that organized religion was an obsolete institution, a crutch, something for people with "weak minds." Aside from the fact that I'd gladly match the minds of people like Martin Buber, Descartes, Ibn-Sina, and Augustine against Mr. Ventura's any day, he couldn't have been more off the mark (or uttered a more worn out, infantile cliché). Fundamentalists and fanatics aside, religious ritual is—or, at its best, should be—for people with open, creative, daring, and adventurous minds. When it's done right it offers a psychic rush like no other, and it transports us to places that most of the time we only dream about.

When religion works, it transcends time and space.

Nobody's advocating that we start slitting the throats of goats and sheep and offering them up as sacrifices again. But fads always pass, while ancient and sometimes arcane traditions, if unearthed, retooled, and made meaningful to our world, are well worth preserving and being given new life. We don't need to reinvent the wheel, or even necessarily construct new models of it. If we'd only look hard enough, we'd come to see that there is enough beauty and relevance buried in our spiritual heritage that old and new, primitive and postmodern, can blend seamlessly into one.

CHAPTER 4

Size Doesn't Matter

The walls and fortifications that encircled Jerusalem had been battered and, in some places, breached. Thousands of Jews had been slaughtered—their bodies were strewn everywhere in various states of decomposition. The alleys and streets were foul with the stench of human waste. Roman troops surrounded the sacred city and its Holy Temple and had completely severed its food and water supply. It was the year 70 C.E., and the long, violent siege of Israel's capital was nearing a bloody and fiery end.

The Romans had come down like a hammer on the Jews, who'd had the audacity four years earlier to revolt against their occupation and its attendant political and religious oppression. Jerusalem was the final refuge, the rebellion's last stand. The Jewish leaders in the besieged city faced stark, grim choices. As in many revolutions, those who favored accommodation or compromise were accused of being traitors. Some were killed. Many chose, out of either conviction or coercion, to side with the revolutionary zealots and fight.

But some looked for another path.

We learn in the Talmud that the religious leader Rabban Yohanan ben Zakkai, after walking through the marketplace during the heat of the siege, sees a group of emaciated men making stew out of straw and fetid water. The zealots, in a strategic ploy to instill in Jerusalem's desperate inhabitants and refugees the belief that they had nothing to lose by fighting, had deliberately burned the meager stores of wheat and barley that still remained within the city's walls. Concerned that the zealots are dangerously misguided and dragging the Jewish people—and the Jewish religion—to the edge of destruction, Rabban Yohanan devises a plan for their spiritual survival.

He invites Abba Sicara, the leader of the zealots, to meet with him in secret. When the commander arrives Rabban Yohanan admonishes him: "How long will you men continue what you are doing? You are killing your own people by famine!" Abba Sicara replies, "What choice do I have? If I dare object to my men, they will kill me." The commander goes on to explain that the zealots have made a pact among themselves not to allow anyone out of the city—except as a corpse.

The rabbi has a response for him, a response that ultimately saves the Jewish people as well as Judaism itself: "Then have *me* taken out as a corpse."

Rabban Yohanan pretends to fall ill and die, and his disciples construct a coffin for him. He is carried beyond the gates of the scarred city and brought to the general Vespasian, who has just been appointed emperor and must now return to Rome. According to legend, Vespasian is impressed with the rabbi's vision and show of wisdom, and he says to the Jewish leader: "I am leaving here and will send someone else [Titus] to take my place. You may, however, make one request of me, and I will grant it." Rabban Yohanan tells the general that he wants to set up a small rabbinical academy in a tiny town: "Give me Yavneh and its sages."

The rabbi does not ask for personal riches or power. What he desires is a gateway to the Jewish future.

The imagery is poignant and paradoxical. Confronted with the death of his people and religion, Rabban Yohanan—by entering a coffin—finds a bridge to renewed life, a path to spiritual resurrection. Though this tale is, in the end, one of survival and success, it always feels sad when I read it. While it is about the passage of Judaism into the rabbinic age, it is also about the sudden, violent end of the biblical era. The Temple is destroyed for the second and final time. Its priests and Levites are murdered. There has been widespread suffering, destruction, and death.

In order for their religious life to continue, Jews had no choice but to change Judaism, to make it transportable, flexible, and imbued with features that would allow it to exist under any conditions and adapt to new contexts and unforeseen situations. In the wake of the bold but failed rebellion against Rome, and after the creation of the school at Yavneh, the rabbinate supplanted the priesthood, the synagogue eclipsed the Temple, and liturgy and prayer replaced animal sacrifice. It was this process of radical transformation and revitalization that restructured Judaism into the form most of us know today.

And this religious revolution was brought about by just one rabbi and his small band of brothers.

The preceding story is one of survival and perseverance. It is also a story about the power and impact of a single individual in the face of overwhelming odds and obstacles. Yet since the Holocaust—and even before that catastrophic event—the Jewish community has been preoccupied with its size (or lack thereof). We have *always* been a religious and cultural minority, enslaved by Egyptians, sandwiched between regional super-powers like Assyria and Babylonia, oppressed by Greeks and Romans.

When the revolt was crushed and the Second Temple was destroyed, a great Diaspora ensued. But Jews remained minorities. Sometimes we were treated well. Other times we were killed. Over time, however, we persevered, even thrived.

When Jews were driven from the land of Israel into exile in Babylonia, many of them prospered in that urban, cosmopolitan society in both the commercial and cultural sectors. More significantly, the small Jewish community established flourishing, world-renowned academies in Sura and Pumpeditha, from which the famous Babylonian Talmud evolved, a codex of sacred texts and dialogues on law and life that continues to be studied by scholars to this day.

Though relatively few in number, the Jews of Muslim Spain generated their own Golden Age during which, over a period of not much more than a century, some of the greatest Jewish thinkers, mystics, poets, and statesmen emerged and influenced the larger medieval world around them for generations. Thomas Aquinas thought so highly of Maimonides, for instance, that he respectfully referred to him in his theological works simply as "the Rabbi."

Clearly, size doesn't matter. What matters is commitment and creativity.

There are scores of other examples that prove this point. So what's our freakin' problem? Why is our organizational leadership obsessed with playing the numbers game, with counting how many potential Jewish babies are lost to our community each year because of intermarriage, or how many Jewish adults slip from the scene as a result of assimilation? Have our mental images of the past made us that insecure? If we had a better grasp of Jewish history—and, along with that knowledge, the insight to reject the warped and inaccurate caricature of the Jewish experience as little more than one horrific calamity after another—then this entire issue would disappear, and we could refocus our energies and initiatives on what really matters.

What best defines us has always been qualitative rather than quantitative. Jews have encountered more obstacles than most other groups, and we overcame them, not by troops or swords, but by fidelity and innovation. As far back as the Bible, the young and diminutive David, long before he became a great king, defeated the Philistine giant, Goliath, on an open battlefield. David emerged unbowed and victorious because he used focus, faith, and fierce determination. The sling and stone that cracked the giant's skull were just extensions of David's will and imagination.

He was the real deal, the original king of gonzo—not the restrained and serene version sculpted by Michelangelo many centuries later that stands today, almost complacently, in Florence. The true David was characterized by a fiery pugnacity, by guts, and by a total refusal to submit to conventional tactics.

He is a metaphor for the kind of Judaism we need now.

The Jewish world is again in a period of intense and ambiguous transition, but there are several contemporary examples of small but dynamic groups and institutions engaged in ambitious efforts to create a meaningful, vigorous Judaism that is relevant for its era and cultural context—and not afraid to challenge assumptions or entrenched orthodoxies. More than connecting Jews with Judaism, these models convey the idea that it is passion, not numbers, that keeps our religion fresh and alive.

One of the more successful, long-lasting, and influential

models is the Brandeis-Bardin Institute, a three-thousand-acre retreat, camp, and cultural center nestled among beautiful, forested hills in the Simi Valley near Los Angeles. It's some of the best Jewish turf outside of Israel.

BBI, in its various incarnations, has been around for a while, and with good reason—many of its innovative ideas and programs have worked, and have made their way into the larger Jewish community. In the early forties, Dr. Shlomo Bardin, a popular Jewish teacher and activist, was extremely concerned (even then, over sixty years ago) about the "accelerating disappearance of young Jews into the American Melting Pot." Bardin didn't want the next Jewish generation to melt away into a multicultural stew. Instead, he wanted Jews to respect other traditions while at the same time learning about, and taking pride in, their own.

Bardin studied the *fokscoler* (folkschool) created in Denmark in the mid-eighteenth century, a model that helped save Danish culture from total German assimilation. He also studied the nascent kibbutz movement in what was then Palestine, and how its system of communal, villagelike living, along with a robust culture of dance, theater, music, and the arts, helped instill a powerful sense of Jewish identity in its members. Bardin hoped to apply many aspects of these models to Jewish life in America and ultimately to reenergize it.

It was a vision shared by U.S. Supreme Court Justice Louis Brandeis, who provided the initial funding for the program's first summer, in 1941. Brandeis died before that summer program began, but his name has been linked to the center ever since.

Despite its modest size and somewhat isolated location, BBI has had a great impact on the Jewish institutional scene and on Jewish leaders around the nation. Long before many of its strategies for reaching out to the disconnected were incorporated into other organizations, Brandeis-Bardin was experimenting with creative approaches to weekend retreats, summer camps, arts and culture events, and informal education. The underlying concept behind all of these efforts was *immersion*.

This is an idea that has become self-evident, with wide-ranging implications. If journalists, for example, need to embed themselves within a battalion in order to better understand a military conflict (as many argue they must), then Jews need to embed themselves within Judaism if they are to better understand, and ultimately identify with, their spiritual heritage.

This strategy of on-the-ground immersion predates the existence of Brandeis-Bardin, and has had perhaps its most obvious impact through the Jewish camping system. The 2000–2001 National Jewish Population Survey I referred to in the first chapter confirmed what had been up until then the conventional wisdom of many Jewish professionals. Despite high rates of intermarriage, low rates of synagogue affiliation, and general disinterest in Jewish religious practice, there are three specific activities that demonstrably engender a sense of Jewish identity more powerfully than any other: enrollment in a Jewish day school; an Israel experience; and attendance at a Jewish summer camp.

All of these involve Jewish immersion of one sort or another. Yet while the growing day school movement is still limited to a mostly traditionalist population, and while large-scale exposure to Israel among our youth (through programs such as Birthright) is still a fairly recent phenomenon, boys and girls have been going to Jewish summer camps for decades. And they can be extremely ideological places—there were, and are, Yiddish camps, Zionist camps, religious camps, secular humanist camps, and camps connected to particular denominations (such as Reform or Conservative Judaism).

Whatever their ideology, these camps have consistently produced Jews who are highly attached to their Jewishness. While the overwhelming majority of Jewish children do not attend Jewish summer camps, the minority who do are very often motivated to become our rabbis, educators, activists, and leaders. And it's had a clear ripple effect. The bonding experience of being surrounded by Jewish peers and saturated with Jewish symbols has undeniably influenced the shape of the wider Jewish community and its most important institutions.

But this bonding and identity-building experience isn't just for kids. Brandeis-Bardin, though it has its own camp program as well, was one of the very first Jewish entities to fully grasp the power of immersion for adults.

Like living (albeit temporarily) in a small village, a BBI retreat is designed to give you a taste, on multiple levels, of a particular subculture—it immerses you in Jewish life. While I was living in Los Angeles during my second year of rabbinical school, I participated in one of their weekend retreats with a group of men and women mainly in their twenties. What I saw and felt blew me away. It reminded me of the time I'd spent as a volunteer on a kibbutz in Israel. From the moment my retreat began on Friday afternoon to its conclusion on Sunday morning, BBI was able, at a single site and with a uniform rhythm, to interweave language, food, education, and worship into a complete Jewish package of culture and community.

You can run, but you can't hide.

What do you do if you're getting ready to work in Paris for a couple of years? Take a French immersion course. From day one, no teacher worth his or her pedagogic salt will let you speak a damn word of English in the classroom.

And what do you do if you want to better understand and appreciate your Jewish heritage? You place yourself in a context where that same cultural and religious heritage is right in your face, wherever you turn, any time of the day or night.

Rabbi Isaac Jeret is a former president of Brandeis-Bardin. For him, the Simi Valley campus is an outreach resource for all Jews, regardless of their age, beliefs, or connection to their identities. "We want to touch and teach," says Jeret. "We don't want to judge. A lot has happened in the Jewish world over the last few decades, and a lot of groups have adopted and adapted our techniques. I take that as a compliment. Before it became as common as it is today, BBI was focused on meeting people where they are, on being nondenominational, on giving Jews the freedom to explore their Jewishness in an open environment. We replaced dogma with debate and even outright rejection. That's why our grasp has been disproportionate to our reach."

By offering the freedom to roam, combined with the paradoxical inescapability of immersion, BBI has a proven track record of producing both lay and religious leaders for the Jewish community.

The kibbutz—Brandeis-Bardin's original institutional paradigm and one often mirrored in the larger network of Jewish camps—affirms the individual by celebrating the collective. It has a very noteworthy track record as well.

It's no accident that for much of the history of the Jewish state, Israel's powerful military drew a disproportionate number of its officer corps from the tiny kibbutz world. A kibbutz, with its tight, interdependent, mainly agrarian culture, fostered and cultivated many of the skills and values that are necessary for good military leadership: a capacity to live and work with others in symbiotic ways; an understanding of how to use

short-term, tactical means to achieve long-term, strategic
goals; an ability to take the initiative and, at times, make tough
decisions; a sense of the importance of self-sacrifice, and a willingness, if necessary, to perform it.

There is a different war being waged in the Jewish community here. But it is one that requires a similar kind of leadership.

How do you fight the colossus of cultural assimilation?
David used devotion and innovation to slay his giant. For Jeret
and BBI, an organization that has always been ahead of the
curve, it is staying ahead of the curve: "We need to make the
next step now and think about Brandeis-Bardin not as a place,
but as a method. While the residential component is absolutely
critical, it is also replicable. Our challenge for this new and unsettling century is to figure out how to export our method elsewhere around the country. Why the hell shouldn't somebody
who lives in Nebraska or North Dakota be able to have a profound experience of total Jewish immersion? You just rent a
facility, hire the right staff, make people aware, and then go
for it."

Slings and stones. Commitment and creativity. It ain't rocket
science, my Jewish brothers and sisters—it's common sense.
The secret to success isn't really a secret at all: Think big but
start small. Know when to be confident and when to be humble. What you need is a great idea (like ethical monotheism), a
great product (like Judaism), and great marketing. It is in this
third, vitally important category that the mainstream Jewish
establishment has failed miserably. At its best, what we have to
offer our community is so wonderful, so powerful, so
enlivening—yet the ways in which we present it are so unimag-
inative and, well, lame.

One theme that's come up repeatedly in this book is the importance of meeting people where they are. Sometimes it means just that—meeting folks, *literally,* where they eat and sleep, work and play, live and breathe.

In the summer of 1993 I traveled alone through the remote Central Asian nations of Kazakhstan, Kyrgyzstan, and Uzbekistan. None of the countries that I visited during my sojourn had even existed until a year earlier, having been predominantly Muslim republics in a now defunct Soviet Union. I was on a self-created humanitarian mission. My goal, inspired in part by the fact that I was only one year away from rabbinic ordination, was to work with several of the isolated and neglected Jewish communities in that region, teaching them about Judaism, bringing books and religious articles, and distributing medicine.

Samarkand (in modern-day Uzbekistan) is one of the oldest cities in the world. It was used as a main stop along the Silk Road as the ancient Greeks transported the exotic treasures of the Far East back to their empire. The Jews of Samarkand, the Bukharans, trace their ancestry to the Babylonian exile. I approached the oasis town on a Friday afternoon, as the Sabbath drew near. My escort and I bought warm loaves of bread with dill and a jar of fresh honey from a roadside vendor for the evening meal we'd have at his home. In the shadow of minarets we drove past the old city, the *mahallah,* winding through the narrow streets and alleyways of the Jewish quarter.

I spotted a man dressed in black and wearing a Hasidic fedora—he looked totally out of place in this Islamic town. We asked if he needed a lift, and picked him up. Since he spoke Hebrew I was able to converse with him (he knew no English and I knew no Russian). It turned out that, like me, he was a Jewish "missionary." He'd been sent to Samarkand for the summer by Chabad-Lubavitch to teach Hebrew to Bukharans who were about to immigrate to Israel. Though

that young man—and the ultra-Orthodox movement that sent
him to Central Asia—was about as different from me in appearance and belief as was possible, I felt a special kinship with
him.

What we shared was a willingness to hit the road, to en-
dure a little hardship, and to travel to the literal margins of the
Jewish world in an attempt to connect with Jews who had
been underserved, or even ignored.

When it comes to reaching the disregarded and disengaged,
Chabad gets it, maybe better than anybody else. They don't just
talk the talk. They're on the ground where Jews are—even hip,
young, searching Jews. I've encountered Chabad emissaries all
over the planet, from the hippie hangouts of Kathmandu,
Nepal, to the rough-and-tumble fishing piers of Ketchikan,
Alaska.

But this is *not* a love letter. It's an acknowledgment of the
group's impact on Jews and Jewish life, and an expression of
some respect.

You better believe I still have a cartload of concerns about
Chabad: the way it twisted its founder's radical mysticism into
a deeply conservative, dynastic system in which its leaders are
treated like royalty and where the last Lubavitcher Rebbe,
Menachem Mendel Schneerson, was widely regarded as a messianic figure, if not the Messiah himself; its literalist view of the
Torah and absolutist take on Jewish tradition; its rejection of
and hostility toward religious pluralism; its extreme parochial-
ism, despite a world filled with problems far removed from
those within the Jewish community; its ultimate but unspoken
objective of converting other Jews to its conformist and narrow
vision of who is a Jew and how a Jew should live.

Yet, damn it, in terms of marketing, Chabad knows what it's
doing, while the rest of us often seem to be groping in the dark
or latching on to the newest fad. While outreach to the discon-

nected has been a hallmark of Chabad's work for decades, many of the mainstream Jewish bureaucracies have been preoccupied with institutional infighting and competitive fundraising. While these organizations were busy sending out boring letters about issues that they deemed pressing to Jews, Chabad was establishing a network of houses on college campuses across the country that offered free Shabbat meals for students who were far from their families, or giving Jewish travelers the chance to celebrate Passover in Prague and other tourist hot spots.

No Jewish group has been more adept at harnessing the power of technology and the media. Despite opposition from other, more cloistered ultra-Orthodox sects, Chabad has been aggressive in its efforts to utilize new methods for marketing its programs. Its Web site is unapologetic: "Everything in this world was created for a divine purpose. All forms of modern technology can and should be harnessed to make the world a better place and, in the case of Jews, to spread Judaism in the widest possible manner." Though all the major Jewish denominations and organizations now have Web sites, Chabad was among the very first and most accessible of them. It's been a venue that has answered questions and provided how-to information for years.

Chabad isn't just accessible—it is visible. Through their high-profile, celebrity telethons (despite the fact that they're hysterically cheesy) and their full-page newspaper announcements on or around Jewish holidays, Chabad uses the various media to make its presence known. It is in your face, and it wants to be. How many of us have run into zealous Chabad members handing out free Shabbat candles on street corners? Or seen their "mitzvah tanks" lumbering through our cities, their bearded, fedora-wearing drivers behind the steering wheels of Winnebagos? Or witnessed, whether we agree with the practice or not, their oversized Chanukah menorahs illuminating our parks and public squares? Why is Chabad, a very small movement numerically, such an enormous success story in so many areas of influence?

With four thousand full-time (rabbinic and lay) emissaries operating around the world, they are accessible—and that makes Judaism accessible.

They offer unconditional acceptance.

They wear their religion on their sleeves, and that can make insecure or tentative Jews feel more at ease with their own Jewish identities.

Though it is self-constructed and self-promotional, they radiate an aura of Jewish authenticity.

They are proud, affirmative, audacious, and, in their own way, unorthodox.

Even though Chabad, like all missionary groups, has a somewhat manipulative agenda (they'd love nothing more than to convert other Jews to their version of Judaism), and though everything above ultimately serves as a means toward fulfilling that agenda, Chabad's techniques and strategies have been studied, copied, and adopted by a large number of other Jewish organizations, religious and secular alike. That in itself testifies to this controversial but emulated movement's inordinate influence.

For faith-based institutions, marketing and fundraising go hand-in-hand, and for generations the primary fundraising organs of North American Jewry have been local "federations" that run annual campaigns to raise money for local social services (mostly, but not exclusively, Jewish), for other local needs (e.g., support of Jewish educational programs), and to aid Jews in Israel and overseas. These federations are affiliated with a national umbrella organization, the United Jewish Communities (UJC), a product of the merger of three predecessor organizations. Each affiliate federation raises money independently, with the help of the national organization, and sends a portion of it to the UJC to go to the overseas recipients. In prior decades, as the Jewish state was going through its birth pangs and development as a nation, the majority of funds went to Israeli rather than to domestic needs.

Today, despite its political problems, Israel has done well enough for itself—and our own Diaspora communities have done so poorly in the areas of Jewish literacy and life—that the distribution has shifted.

The various federations and the UJC have done, and continue to do, great work: They support community centers, schools, outreach programs, hospitals, new immigrants. Yet in recent years, some American Jews—particularly those with means and strong philanthropic impulses—have wanted to have a much more active say in, and far more control over, how their money is spent. This has led to the cracking of an unwritten code, and some of the country's wealthiest Jewish funders and families have either decreased or ceased their charitable contributions to the federation network, earmarked their gifts for only certain areas within the UJC orbit, or set up their own foundations with their own agendas.

To be sure, some of these private foundations are vanity projects, extensions of the oversized egos of corporate CEOs, industrial magnates, and hedge-fund titans. Unfortunately, we Jews have our share of Donald Trump figures, and their names are emblazoned on buildings and letterheads. While their hair (if they still have any) might look better, not much else about them is very different.

Others are far more serious about their philanthropy, and there is clearly an emerging minimovement. Significantly, some of the most influential of these philanthropists aren't the

richest, but they are the most innovative. One especially imaginative and successful phenomenon that has emerged from
these independent philanthropists has been the creation of "incubators," parent organizations who, through funding and
other forms of support, help to nurture and eventually launch
start-up groups that are geared toward younger, disconnected
Jews and headed by dynamic Jewish entrepreneurs and social
engineers.

Martin Kaminer and his family have been at the forefront
of this effort. But Kaminer has always believed that the path to
communal transformation won't be found through petty, self-
righteous antagonism, but instead through thoughtful, strategic partnership. In 2000, Kaminer, along with the UJC and
JESNA (the Jewish Education Service of North America),
founded Bikkurim: An Incubator for New Jewish Ideas.

"It was a no-brainer," says Kaminer. "I was at a meeting
where the president of the UJC stood up and proclaimed that
they wanted to infuse—through one orifice or another—their
venerable institution with new ideas. So I decided to call his
bluff. The UJC wanted some spiritual Viagra, and there were
all these talented, young entrepreneurial Jews out there in
need of support and guidance to get their personal projects off
the ground. Each offered something to the other. My family
just served as the middleman. We saw our role as helping to
connect seasoned, somewhat tired professionals with hungry
young visionaries."

And what would be the goal of the collaboration?

Kaminer goes on: "By connecting hot young idealists with
experienced and dedicated 'Jewrocrats,' Bikkurim—which
means 'first fruits,' the most valuable of biblical offerings—
would help to nourish and energize *both* groups. Everybody
would be in each other's face. They'd walk the same halls and
use the same stalls. We'd create a kind of organic process of

cross-fertilization that would be beneficial, ultimately, to the Jewish community at large."

The Bikkurim plan, which has led in only ten years to the cultivation of over thirty brand-new Jewish organizations in varying stages of development, was to mix old and new under one roof—the roof, literally, of the UJC offices in Manhattan. Bikkurim has provided its start-ups with free office space, technical assistance, access to professional and organizational networks, and counsel from experts in relevant fields through residencies that can last up to almost five years.

A few examples of these start-ups are as impressive as they are diverse:

Heeb: A quarterly national magazine of alternative Jewish life, politics, art, culture, and spirituality, with a target audience of Jews in their twenties and thirties. *Heeb* interweaves Jewish identity and urban secular culture with modern, flashy, and edgy pictures and articles. The magazine also sponsors entertainment through special events.

JDub Records: A nonprofit record label and production company for new Jewish music. The group works to redefine Jewish music, help connect Jews to a deeper understanding of their Judaism, and spread new visions of Jewish culture. JDub fosters positive Jewish identity and builds community among younger Jews through music and musical events.

Hazon: A group whose mission is to bring people together—irrespective of age, denomination, or background—to learn, celebrate, and make a difference. Hazon is rooted in Jewish tradition but focused on the future. Its particular interest is in the area of Jewish environmental and outdoor education. It holds multi-day environmental bike rides in the United States and Israel.

MATAN: The Gift of Jewish Learning for Every Child: A multidisciplinary team of educators, specialists, and mental health professionals committed to providing Jewish education to children with special learning needs. MATAN works with Jewish day schools and supplemental schools, designing curricula and consulting with classroom teachers.

The New Shul: My own congregation, which I've described a bit in this book. Were it not for Bikkurim, who took us in when others in the Jewish world turned us away, we might never have made it.

Though Bikkurim is an East Coast initiative, there was, from 2000 to 2005, a West Coast expression of the incubator concept. It was called Joshua Venture, and it was formed by a triumvirate of independent family foundations. Like Bikkurim, Joshua Venture helped to nurture new and promising Jewish organizations, but it was also interested in leadership training, and it awarded two-year fellowships to creative Jewish social entrepreneurs and engineers between the ages of twenty-one and thirty-five. (I led a group of them on a rock-climbing trip in the Delaware Water Gap and can testify to their talent.) While Joshua Venture has re-emerged and is now entering into a new stage of its existence, its West Coast legacy lives on through the innovative spin-off organizations that emerged from it and that have touched young lives.

Many of the groups that were helped by Joshua Venture and Bikkurim are now active and important, and some have been incorporated into larger organizations. A few never made it through their incubation period to a state of self-sufficiency; some dissolved for other reasons. Yet both Jewish incubators were willing to take risks on unknown quantities and to try to turn their visions into realities. These two initiatives broke from the pack and ran with their idea, allowing other young Jews to run with theirs. While relatively modest in their scope, they've had a significant impact on the wider Jewish community that continues, and that proves the equally significant point that size is—and very frequently has been—irrelevant to Jewish strength and vitality.

It's too soon to tell how long-lasting their impact will be on the American Jewish community, but if they stay true to their courses, don't pander to the young and try too hard to be hip, and use common sense, these and other efforts should succeed.

Here's a proviso: Size might not mean much, but you can run into problems when the wrong people get their hands on a disproportionate amount of power and influence. Many of the philanthropic fat cats, for instance, know absolutely nothing about Judaism and have a completely inadequate perspective on Jewish history. Some don't want to bother to learn. It's no wonder, then (since a number of these very wealthy men and women had crappy experiences in Hebrew school or with a rabbi when they were kids), that there is a strong antisynagogue and anticlerical bent to many of the projects that they sponsor and support. Do we really want adults who can't get over their childhood baggage about religion calling the shots about the future of Jewish life?

Just because you know how to run a multinational corporation, or can make billions of dollars in the stock market, doesn't mean you know diddly about what our current Jewish community truly needs in order to move forward.

A related problem is the tendency of many of today's Jewish organizations and foundations to apply rigid, universal business models to *religious* institutions and projects. Non-profits certainly need to keep their fiscal books in order, and they clearly need to promote their programs and services, but the goals of a spiritual community are not—and should not be—the same as that of a financial institution. The job of Walt Disney is to make money for its shareholders. The job of Judaism (and its attendant support systems, such as the synagogue) is to educate and elevate our God-given souls, but also to challenge us to feed the hungry, clothe the naked, redeem the captive, pursue justice, and mend a broken world.

All the groups and initiatives in this chapter have had powerful impacts disproportionate to their sizes. In their willingness to take risks, they stand apart from much of the Jewish crowd. And they offer important, replicable models to those of us on the outside as well. So if a formal retreat center isn't your thing, rent a cabin or two in a state park with some friends and hold a do-it-yourself Jewish Weekend in the Woods. If cultural institutions don't rock your boat, invite over a group of guests to discuss the latest Jewish book or film in the comfort of your living room. Or, on the philanthropic front, have your family partner up with another one and fund your own social action cause or entrepreneurial project.

Our obsession with numbers is rooted in fear and self-pity, in our sense of being in a perpetual state of peril, but our own history suggests that such fear is unfounded. Brash, bold, sometimes irreverent strategies for reimagining our religion, our spiritual identities, and our concept of community should be our current focus. That is what will lead to our survival and vitality. If the Jewish mainstream and its leadership disagree, let 'em. They're misguided, and they almost always have been.

During the Passover Seder we read a famous verse from the Torah that has a lot to teach us about the path to communal growth: "My father was a wandering Aramean. He went down to Egypt, few in number, and sojourned there. And there he became a great nation" (Deuteronomy 26:5). The patriarch Jacob—also known as Israel and a symbol of the Jewish people as a whole—recounts the Exodus story with a mixture of humility and pride. He is the son of a nomad, a member of a clan. Yet he is also a link in a chain that stretches across generations, a chain that transcends time and place.

Start small, think big.

Our tiny ancestral band of nomadic tribes became a mighty nation and brought monotheism to the world—but only after years of struggle and sacrifice.

No Egypt can destroy a faithful people's ferocious will to live.

No prison can constrain creative minds determined to break free.

CHAPTER 5

Give Tents a Chance:
A Second Look at Tribalism

A COUPLE OF YEARS AGO I TRAVELED with my brother, mostly on horseback, through northwestern Mongolia, a remote region of herdsmen and nomads. Yet now that I've been back in New York City for quite some time—an urban environment that seems about as *un*nomadic as you can get—our exotic journey through those mountains and steppes somehow feels increasingly relevant to my life and my mission as a rabbi. That experience of tribalism, of community at its most raw, intimate, and intense, affected me very deeply, and offered me important lessons that have much to teach American Jewry as our generation enters this next unsettling century.

Within the first few days of our journey—after passing herds of camels, yaks, and goats, and traversing the habitat of ibex, wolves, and endangered snow leopards—we came across a celebration. A young man was about to be married, and relatives and neighbors from the surrounding area had gathered in a collective effort to build him a *ger*—a circular, transportable, tentlike structure that helped Genghis Khan conquer much of the world—as a wedding present.

When we arrived and were invited to participate in the construction of the *ger,* the *ger* itself was about half-finished— its wooden frame and central posts stood bare, like a skeleton, awaiting the flesh of felt that would soon envelop and protect this new home. The men used hammers, saws, and sinews to build and affix the frame, while the women scraped the felt covering that would shelter the young couple from the weather of the northern steppes.

I tried my best to do my part, which consisted mostly of schmoozing through a translator with the groom's father and uncles and taking photos of the children. Since my brother and I had to leave the event in order to move on with our own trip, this cultural experience concluded with a midafternoon feast of candy and homemade cheese curds, followed by cele-bratory toasts of vodka and fermented mare's milk.

Never before had I felt so welcomed, even as a total stranger, into somebody else's world—*their* party had become *our* party.

This powerful communitarian sensibility is related as much to necessity as it is to morality. No one in that world could have survived without the active help of others. What I saw was a form of humanitarian aid that wasn't institutional or solicited, but commonplace and expected.

One of the great nomads in the biblical tradition is Abra-ham. And there's a narrative in the book of Genesis that is of-ten used to illustrate Abraham's morality and to serve as a model for how we, too, should behave toward others. Three mysterious strangers unexpectedly appear in the desert and approach the tent of Abraham and Sarah. Rather than reach for a weapon, the patriarch rushes out to greet them and in-vites them into his home for food and shelter.

It's clear that Abraham and his wife had an "open tent" policy—a policy that, in a nomadic and tribal culture, was related not just to an ethical code, but to survival. What I saw in Mongolia afforded me an unforgettable glimpse into that world of Abraham and Sarah, the world of the nomad. While that society isn't a perfect one, it does inculcate a culture of the open tent, of hospitality and interdependence. What tribal culture does, and does so effectively, is wash away the illusion of self-reliance, the myth of independence and individualism that so many of us Americans have bought into for so many years— more now, arguably, than ever before. It shows us the lunacy of trying to go it alone, and the truth that we don't have to.

Like the institutions of science, technology, and government, tribalism has both positive and negative dimensions. The tribal culture I bore witness to was one of selflessness and interdependence. It was one that held the values of community and commitment above all else. In sharp contrast, ours is a culture of narcissism, of extreme and excessive individualism, of the radical pursuit of our own needs and personal desires—and, on the global level, of unilateralism.

Self-worship is our generation's sin.

What is it, then, that we need to atone for in modern America? Not for having packed up our tents and moved into townhouses. Not for having traded in our camels and horses for cars and planes. But for having, in the process, abandoned our commitment to a culture of community.

With most of the external structures of tribalism gone, how can we regain its *internal* ones, its core values and virtues? This is the challenge of modernity itself. If we fail to overcome, or even face, this existential struggle, then we will have failed in our humanity—we will have taken the gift that is our birthright, the gift of Abraham and Sarah's open tent, and sealed its entrance shut.

And when we seal the entrance to that sacred tent, we seal the entrance to our hearts.

The narcissistic impulses so prevalent today are only the outer crust of our hidden worlds—they are this society's mask. Beneath that mask, in those murky regions of our souls that we're too afraid to confront honestly, we are needier than ever. We live in an era of disturbing violence and roiling hatreds, of color-coded terror alerts, of alienation from those around us as well as from our own families. We live during a dark period in time, and its evolution is uncertain and unsettling.

As a Jew, I come from a nation of nomads, of free spirits. Ours is a tribal religion with tribal roots. Most of the answers to society's current problems—our fears, anxieties, and feelings of loneliness—aren't in self-help books or weekend getaways, but in our own, sometimes primal, spiritual heritage. Judaism offers correctives, pathways that allow us to regain the elemental values our culture so desperately needs and the anchors of authentic community we so deeply crave.

There are many rites and rituals—we've looked at some already—that can help us improve our moral characters and cultivate a more harmonious, truly compassionate community, society, and world. But for this to happen we have to accept one of the first rules of tribal life: The motivation for our behavior must be grounded, not necessarily in what we *want* to do, but in what we *ought* to do.

Today, that's a brazenly countercultural idea.

Tradition states that Abraham's tent was exposed to every direction—it was welcoming, but it made him vulnerable. And that's precisely the point: It is only through vulnerability that genuine community can emerge, that commitment and compassion become intertwined and inseparable.

Both require a risk on our part. Both necessitate that we make a leap of faith beyond our normal comfort zone.

Modernity gives tribalism a very bad rap. Part of why most of us look down on tribal religions or religiously motivated groups is the result of what we see around us, events that we associate with more primitive mind-sets and cultures: the violence in the Balkans; the bloodshed in Chechnya and Sudan; the terrorism of the radical Islamists. To most of us tribalism means feuding and fighting, ethnocentricity and triumphalism, "insiders" and "outsiders," closed-mindedness.

But it doesn't have to. It is usually only when political or personal agendas (or vendettas) get mixed up with social or spiritual ones that such horrific problems occur. If we look deeper—and see tribalism at its best and most authentic rather than at its worst and most distorted—it has much to teach us.

Signs of an emerging tribalism are everywhere. But it's too soon to tell if it will lead to a renewed sense of community or just more conflict and separatism.

The intense pressures of contemporary life, profound insecurity, and ever-worsening social fragmentation and confusion have caused a terrible longing for old certainties and reassuring fantasies. That's where we see the turn toward tribalism most clearly and passionately now, and in some of its most problematic, troubling forms: fundamentalism and fantasism.

Fundamentalist religion (as seen, to take just one recent example, through the Taliban in Afghanistan) is, ironically, a modern phenomenon. While medieval Islamic thinkers opened their minds and debated the issues of their day in elegant, blue-tiled *madrasas* (Koranic schools), today's militant Islamic ideologues bring their "us versus them" concerns to the streets and view their sometimes homicidal actions as appropriate responses to—and even a mandated holy war against—the individualistic, secular, hedonistic, infidel culture of the

West. Disregarding the example of our shared patriarch Abraham (or Ibrahim, to Muslims), the first instinct of this movement is not to reach out a hand in fellowship, but to reach for an AK-47.

A different and far less damaging expression of the tribal impulse can be found among Westerners themselves, in fantasist experiments like Burning Man. This one-week spectacle of art, music, and back-to-the-land living takes place in the Black Rock Desert of Nevada, and it has grown quickly from a spontaneous gathering at a small San Francisco beach into an international convocation that draws over twenty-five thousand zealots. While Burning Man's organizers boast about the formation of their annual but transitory creative community, the overarching focus of the event, as is clearly evident from its Web site and literature, is on self-expression, self-reliance, and self-actualization—not on the self-transcendence that defines classical tribalism.

While these outer manifestations of the tribal impulse are not even remotely analogous, their inner motivations are similar, even understandable—a craving to find one's place, a yearning to unload repressed, primal urges that mainstream religion hasn't made possible, a rejection of many aspects of modern life.

Yet fundamentalism and fantasism represent tribalism gone wrong. Authentic, organic tribalism is rooted in *inter*dependence, not independence, in openness, not isolation. It is certainly not driven by the desire to combat or escape from the world we live in through organized and fiery outbursts of violence or emotionalism—it is driven by the desire to live in harmony *with* our world, flawed and fractured though it may be.

That's a lot harder to do. Ask the nomads I met in Mongolia.

Is modern tribalism ever justified? Are there good models out there that avoid the pitfalls of the two examples above?

Moving beyond the self, in this day and age, is uncomfortable—but that's what it's all about. Yeah, carving a tattoo into your butt and piercing your eyelid may have some loose links to a fantastical tribal past, but are they really going to do squat to help create a better society? Many of us want to tap into our more primitive souls, to be freed, if only temporarily, from the frenetic hyperculture that often constricts and confines us. That's fine. But we've got to separate the superficial from the serious.

Are we in search of true community (and willing to work for it), or do we just want attention?

People change cities, jobs, and social settings constantly. One consequence of this new historical phenomenon is the appearance that nothing is fixed and that everything is choice. In the past, when it came to group identification (whether it took a national, ethnic, or religious form), a person had little say in the matter—you were simply born into a tribe or a community, and that's pretty much where you stayed. Things couldn't be more different now. We've shifted from a culture of *descent* to one of *consent*. Modernity, in a radical break with primeval tradition, has provided us with the capacity to choose our own tribe, our own group identity.

Is that a blessing or a burden? I think it's a bit of both.

Modern tribalism is still in the process of inventing itself—it is still a work in progress, trying to find the right balance between embracing community and cultivating individuality. Sometimes that leads to silly or even reckless stabs in the dark. Other times it leads to deep transformation.

A colleague of mine believes that many of us today are on quests to find "lost tribes of the mind," affiliations that come from emotional or philosophical connections rather than out of necessity or birthright. But why are we looking for these connections? Because ultimately we all want to belong, to feel a meaningful relationship with that which surrounds us, even if only momentarily. Contemporary society, especially here in the West, rarely provides us with that kind of feeling. Instead, it keeps us looking for bigger and better things—which makes it very difficult to feel connected to where we are or fulfilled by who we are.

The tribal impulse is our hunger for the most elemental of connections and sensations.

What does Judaism have to say about tribalism? A lot. The early Israelites were made up of nomadic tribes, and their faith was rooted in tribal values—where community and compassion were paramount, where interdependence was the rule and survival mechanism, where people did things not because they wanted to but because they were supposed to. Our Israelite ancestors made decisions not based on their needs alone, but by taking into consideration the needs of others as well.

Long after their desert wanderings, and following the period of the Temple, historical events changed "Israelites" into "Jews." Yet even in the new world of their Diaspora communities, Jews retained the core teachings of tribal life through their reshaped, urbanized religion. The importance of interdependence, for instance, was lifted from its original nomadic setting and transposed onto a more sedentary foundation. Tribalism became metaphor and myth. It was, and is, transmitted through prayer and practice, holidays and holy books.

But tribalism, particularly in its religious context, isn't just about community. It's about the rituals and rites that help to *create* community.

A classic—and, for some, very controversial—example of one such primitive rite of passage in the Jewish religion is circumcision. While tattoos, as defacements of our bodies for the sake of personal expression, were forbidden in the Bible, ritual circumcision (*bris* in Yiddish and *brit milah* in Hebrew) was deemed acceptable because it was perceived as a permanent sign that marked an individual Jew's identification with the Jewish tribe, and a symbol of his fidelity and commitment to the *brit,* the Covenant—a sacred code and eternal bond between God and other human beings.

Circumcision is not a glorification of the self, but of spiritual community.

Why does this rite roil the emotions of so many? It's designed to. The *brit* ritual has been around for many centuries, and for good reason: It holds tremendous power. Traditions come and go. The ones that stick around almost always survive because they're the ones that work, and because they transcend the limitations of time and place. As a rabbi who has taken part in dozens of such life-cycle ceremonies, I've witnessed it all. I've seen mothers leave the room or faint, fathers grimace or smile, grandparents weep with pride or joy or the recovery of distant memories.

Brit milah is a jarring rite. Drawing blood isn't an option— it's a requirement. But the shock of bloodshed, and how that shock affects us, is exactly the point. These ancient rites should be embraced in all their primitivism, not rationalized away by our modern minds. Sure, there's an element of pain involved. But that element is key to the elemental power of this tribal practice. How often does a typical synagogue service really stir our passions in the ways that we so frequently wish it would? The ability of the *brit* ceremony to foster familial bonds and naked spirituality is rarely, if ever, found in contemporary institutional religion.

But it only works when we let down our walls.

Normative Judaism, despite its historic capability to transport and transform, is presented today in a manner that far too often waters down its magic, its capacity to enchant. It has been neutered of the sense of wonderment that we crave and that serves as a prerequisite for transcendent experience. Modern tribalism is an attempt to remedy this problem and to give us the kind of nourishment we need. When we strip away the exoskeleton of mainstream religion and dive into its primordial guts, we take ourselves back to a much more basic form of connection with the spiritual, one that occurs on a much more overt physical level.

Not dogma or doctrine, but fire and blood—*these* are the tools of the tribe.

The *brit milah* ritual (as well as a wide range of other practices), in and of itself, demonstrates very clearly that you don't need to run off to a fundamentalist training camp in Afghanistan, or flee to a fantasist festival in the Nevada desert, in order to find the raw, sometimes unruly power of tribalism. It's alive and well in our own religious backyard. Maybe not in the Judaism we see around us most of the time, and maybe not in the Judaism of our parents or grandparents. But the Lion of Judah is there, waiting to be unleashed, in the rich and nourishing soil of our past. It's the nexus between the modern and the ancient, the conduit from the physical to the metaphysical.

In the first chapter I discussed how important it is for us to get out of our heads and into our hearts and souls. But a gonzo approach to Jewish life demands that we get into our bodies as well—and tribalistic rituals help us to do that with startling effectiveness. If we are to construct a leaner and meaner Judaism, spirituality and physicality must work hand in hand. We need to be lean: Our rituals have to be stark, exposed, stripped to the bone. That's what makes them accessible. And we've got to be mean: Those institutions that are too remote, uninspiring, or irrelevant must be cast out from our camp the way a tough editor crosses out useless words from a manuscript.

There will certainly be times when we'll want more elaborate rites, like the multisensory Celebration of the Drawing of the Waters. But simplicity and minimalism have their place in Judaism as well.

We shouldn't underestimate the ability of tribalism's external symbols and practices to affect us in profound, emotional ways. The various elements of tribal religious expression—many of which are shared and utilized by faiths other than Judaism—tend to be more palpable and physical in nature than those found in commonplace forms of religious observance. Blood is an essential part of the *brit* ceremony, as described above. But there are several other key ingredients to many, if not most, tribalistic practices: fire, sound (often involving simple percussive instruments, like drums), and dance are among the most typical.

This isn't arbitrary or accidental. All of them are intended to make inroads into, and help animate, our bodies.

With fire, our bodies feel heat. With drums, our bodies are touched by vibrations, like the pulsations of a heart. With dance, our bodies move. If we can't let down our walls, these very sensory, very physical rituals will *break* them down.

Historically, the *brit milah* ritual has often been observed in private homes. But another powerful Jewish ritual with rich tribal roots, Lag B'Omer, has become, of necessity, an outdoor, public event. Though it is a minor holiday in Judaism and not widely known by the mainstream Jewish community, it has been revived in some quarters, particularly in Israel, and its primitive and elemental character has, in compelling ways, been recaptured. More than any other sacred Jewish day, Lag B'Omer mirrors several of the trends in the movement toward a modern tribalism.

The seven weeks between Passover (the commemoration of the Exodus from Egypt) and Shavuot (the celebration of the giving of the Torah at Mount Sinai) are known as the time of the counting of the Omer, an ancient form of measurement. Originally, and when the Temple stood, this was a period associated with harvest festivities in the land of Israel. It was a time of joyful anticipation, a kind of mystical bridge between the Israelites' moment of liberation and their moment of revelation fifty days later. While the Exodus marked the physical birth of the Jewish nation, God's gift of the Torah represented the *spiritual* birth of this wandering people—and the completion, in that sense, of their journey.

Lag B'Omer is the thirty-third day in this countdown period. It took on special significance in Judaism only after the Second Temple was destroyed. In 135 C.E. there was yet another Jewish revolt against Roman occupation, this one led by a charismatic Jewish warrior named Bar Kochba. It ended disastrously, and legend has it that it was during the Omer period that the students of Rabbi Akiva, one of Judaism's greatest sages and an initial supporter of Bar Kochba, died of a strange, unknown plague. The counting of the Omer thus became associated not with celebration, but with sadness. In traditional Jewish communities to this day, weddings, music, and haircuts are not permitted during this time of semimourning.

After the decimation of his students, Rabbi Akiva had cultivated new disciples, and his greatest, according to lore, was Rabbi Shimon bar Yochai, viewed by some mystics (though disputed by contemporary scholars) as the author of the Zohar, the central text of classical Kabbalah. Lag B'Omer is treated both as the *yartzeit* (or anniversary) of his death and the day on which he revealed the secret meanings of his mysterious text. In a different tradition, this day is also connected with the date that Bar Kochba's army won a major military victory by temporarily retaking Jerusalem, adding a nationalist dimension to the event, particularly as it is observed in the modern state of Israel. Each tradition explains and allows for a one-day break in the solemn, sorrowful Omer period.

That break has evolved into a primal eruption of tribal ritual and emotion.

The Lag B'Omer celebration at Mount Meron in northern Israel illustrates this phenomenon more clearly than any other in the world—and makes Burning Man look like a bunch of schoolchildren playing in a sandbox. In the spring, on the thirty-third day of the countdown toward Shavuot, 250,000 people gather on and around this Galilean mountain. All the tribalistic elements are present: fire, music, dance, even blood. Men and women from Israel and abroad, in a modern act of pilgrimage, congregate there in clusters. Some visit the tomb of Rabbi Shimon bar Yochai himself, which is situated at Mount Meron, to pay homage to and pray ecstatically beside the bones of this Kabbalistic giant.

Judaism teaches that the souls of the righteous ascend to heaven upon liberation from their bodies, so it isn't as odd as it might seem that the anniversary of this Kabbalist's death has become an occasion to rejoice with raw abandon. There is feasting and fervor. During the day people have picnics, drink homemade arrack, and dance to the beat of drum machines and electronic keyboards. Some slaughter live lambs and barbecue the skewered meat right on the spot. In one folk custom, hundreds of three-year-old boys have their hair ritually cut for the first time. At night torches are lit and towers of wood are set aflame, with some bonfires reaching twenty or thirty feet toward the sky, dispelling the darkness.

The entire Mount Meron area is blanketed with humanity and crackling with sparks and fire.

In mainstream Judaism fire is essential, but it is used

mostly in a subdued way, with candles, to usher in holy days or to honor the memories of departed loved ones. In expressions of Jewish tribalism (such as Lag B'Omer), fire is allowed to burn without restraint, and its symbolism becomes far more powerful. For the serious celebrants at Mount Meron, the columns of flame around them might represent the fire that accompanied the revelation at Mount Sinai, or the illuminating, mystical light of the Zohar, or the passionate striving of our souls to reunite with their divine source. With respect to Rabbi Shimon bar Yochai's "presence" during the event, fire might also recall a teaching from the Mishnah: "Warm yourself by the fire of the sages."

But not everybody who comes to Mount Meron is serious—not everyone who journeys to the Galilee is in search of spiritual communion or community.

For many, Lag B'Omer is just an excuse to party. Or to make money. Like Burning Man, it attracts hucksters as well as holy men, teens on Ecstasy as well as true ecstatics. That's one of the dangers of modern tribalism: Its external enticements often mask a hollow (and crassly commercial) heart. As you roam the grounds of Mount Meron, you can see how so much of it has become a shtickfest: There are vendors peddling mystical amulets, blessed bottles of mountain spring water, and decks of "rebbe cards" alongside booths that offer pilgrims cigarette lighters, boiled corn, and baklava. It sometimes feels more like a carnival than a sacred festival.

What draws so many thousands of people? Are tribal events like these driven by base, bacchanalian urges, or by the desire to create genuine community?

My guess is it's an unconscious combination of both.

Yet for it to be true to its roots, *Jewish* tribalism must be grounded, not in neopagan pyrofetishism, but in monotheism. We should certainly let loose, and there's nothing wrong with partying hard, but we can't allow ourselves to lose sight of the real object of our wilder, less tamed celebrations: *God,* and the sparks of God that are within each and every one of us.

When those elements are brought into alignment with one another, we will find everything that we all ultimately long for: spirituality, community, and authenticity.

I've been very fortunate, both as a rabbi and an adventure-travel junkie, to have traveled through some stunning and re-mote regions of the world, where I have been able to observe genuine tribalism firsthand—as well as the values associated with its historic and healthy manifestations. In Central Asia I've dined and dialogued with Kazakh, Kyrgyz, and Uzbek men and women; in the northern Caucasus I've been hosted by Ossetians (who practice an ancient form of religion that in-volves the ritual sacrifice of rams) and sipped tea with Balkar-ians and Kabardins; and I've experienced the warmth of Mongolians, riding their horses and sleeping on the floors of their *gers.*

The rites and rituals that are interwoven into these com-munities also interweave the sacred and the secular—there's no real distinction between the two. But these particularistic observances are meant to serve a larger purpose: They are a means to an end. Opening your tent to a stranger (whether that tent is actual or metaphorical) is an obligation in these cultures, plain and simple. The ritual acts connected with it might involve an exchange of gifts or the drinking of mare's milk, but the hospitality they engender and convey is univer-sal. That core value doesn't make you more spiritual or ethi-cal. It just makes you a responsible member of the tribe.

This kind of expansive religion in the raw, something we rarely witness in the West, isn't what we usually have in mind when we think about Judaism.

But it sure as hell ought to be. Tribalistic expression in today's society can be both a rebellion against the present Jewish status quo and—simultaneously—a radical return to our more primitive roots.

That's why the gonzo Jew frequently feels out of place—and sometimes even marginalized—within organized Judaism. Like a stranger in a strange land.

And we're not the first generation of Jews to feel this way.

Back in the sixties, Jewish hippies—hostile toward organized religion but hungry to experiment with alternative paths in which to express their Jewish identities and spirituality—flirted with certain aspects of tribalism as well. Yet while some of these disaffected and alienated young Jews ran off to join desert communes in an attempt to recapture that more elemental lifestyle, others founded the *havurah* movement. Their focus wasn't on large-scale, public events, but instead on private, internal structures, on the creation of intimate communities.

Designed like a tightly knit tribe—or at least their romanticized conception of how an authentic tribe was structured—these *havurot* (often made up of fewer than a dozen people) were nonhierarchical in nature, egalitarian, participatory, and consensus-based in the way they made decisions, and completely transparent in everything from their budgets to their personal lives. Household chores and other daily or weekly responsibilities were shared collectively. Members (or *haverim* in Hebrew) worked together, lived together, ate together, slept together.

Like a kibbutz or a retreat center, each *havurah* provided a unique immersion experience where time, environment, even diet (most were kosher) were kept in tune with Jewish rhythms and in line with Jewish practices.

Since a *havurah* was a particular kind of commune—a Jewish one—religious ritual was an integral part of the community's life. True to the zeitgeist of the sixties, and in rejection of the huge establishment synagogues and stuffy services that most of the movement's founders grew up with, a typical *havurah* service was both intimate and informal. At a Shabbat service, for example, you'd see people relaxing in jeans on the floor or on pillows, sometimes slapping drums and sometimes strumming guitars. There was no service leader per se—everybody participated in leading the service through songs, prayers, and readings.

In keeping with its nonhierarchical, tribal tradition, the *havurah* movement was outspokenly anticlerical. Rabbis were welcome to join a service, but they held no special status in the community when it came to officiating at life-cycle ceremonies or transmitting Jewish teachings. Ironically, several of the baby-boomer founders of this movement have since become some of today's leading rabbis themselves.

The *havurah* movement was small but influential. Many of its ideas and approaches (such as participatory services, egalitarianism in ritual and liturgical language, and the incorporation of instrumentation—beyond the pipe organ—into worship) have become standard in a great number of congregations across the country.

Havurot are still around. And some continue to exist in independent, stand-alone forms. But in an interesting and positive development, many of them have emerged from *within* synagogues. Recognizing that it's absolutely impossible to create a feeling of intimacy, fellowship, and genuine community in a twenty-five-hundred-household "battleship" congregation, some of the more innovative rabbis and lay leaders in Jewish life have actively promoted the concept of what I call "embedded *havurot.*"

With this model, subgroups of eight or ten families, couples, and/or singles create, in essence, their own *havurah,* yet still remain connected to their larger home institution. These

much more intimate groups meet regularly to socialize, celebrate holidays, and explore shared interests. Like clans in a
tribe, some of these *havurot* have become extended families for
their members.

In the end, I think this is only a temporary solution to our
edifice complex and our inane preoccupation with size. But it's
a start. (Although Jews are a small percentage of America's total population, many of our congregations are on the larger
side. Maybe one reason is that our insecurity and siege mentality compel those of us who do affiliate with a synagogue to
seek a sense of safety in numbers.)

There *is* a problem with the *havurah* model, and it's a problem I've experienced myself. It's directly related to the far
more serious—and, as history demonstrates, at times lethal—
dark side of tribalism in general.

I spent the year after my college graduation living in Cam-
bridge, Massachusetts, and writing the Great (and, thank God,
never published) American Novel. It was also a year in which I
struggled as a young Jew to find a spiritual home—a struggle
that would ultimately result in my decision to enter the rabbinate. Someone I knew and trusted suggested that I try the
Shabbat services at Havurat Shalom in nearby Somerville, one of
the very first *havurot* in the nation and a residential Jewish community that had stayed in existence since its founding in 1968.

Though the services were decent—lots of singing, heavily
participatory—the experience as a whole was not. From the
moment I entered the house and sat down by myself on a pillow, it was clear to me that there was a sharp, and deliberate,
distinction between visitors and members. No one had to say a
word; body language said it all. Nobody sat next to me, shook
my hand, or even smiled in acknowledgment of my presence.
No one directed me to the table in the dining room to join the
group for the Sabbath meal when services had ended.

I might have been in a "tent," but its flaps had been only partially opened for me. I felt little warmth, just an alienating aura of clannishness. There was an Us and there was a Them, and I was definitely one of Them.

So much for back-to-basics Jewish hospitality.

I got over my hurt feelings and bruised ego, but the episode stuck with me. Taken to its logical extension and most extreme form, it is just this sort of tribalistic, exclusionary mindset and behavior that can easily lead to antipathy between individuals and groups, and, in its worst-case scenario, to violence.

If this is community, I recall thinking, *who wants any damn part of it?*

Sure, the *havurah* had no walls—but only for those who were already tucked safely within the fortress.

All this talk of tribalism and tribal culture resurrects for me another memorable experience I had during my trip to Mongolia.

Late one day, as the sun had begun to set, two strangers and their horses (all of whom seemed to have appeared out of thin air) suddenly approached our camp. They'd been riding for three days and nights, searching for their lost herd of seventeen camels. As we spoke with them over dinner, we learned that they'd been traveling through the high desert without any food or supplies. To eat and sleep they had been stopping at *ger*s as they passed, and had always been invited in for a place to sleep on a rug, or for a meal—just as they were now doing with us.

The acculturated Westerner in me thought, *How very Tennessee Williams of them—these herdsmen are truly dependent on the kindness of strangers.* Yet, on further reflection, I came to realize that the provisions and shelter they received weren't really an expression of kindness, and the people who took them in weren't really strangers, even if they'd never met them before. In their context and culture those ideas didn't exist as they do for us. It was all a matter of survival, and a radically broadened sense of what constitutes genuine community.

There was no stark barrier between Us and Them, Ours and Yours. In their world, what goes around will, and must, come around.

When we awoke in our camp the next morning, the herdsmen and their horses were gone—no good-byes, no handshakes, nothing. We made coffee and ate breakfast. It was cold and hazy—the steppes afforded no protection from the wind and mist blowing over the mountain lake in front of us. Soon, though, the sun began to rise higher. As our bodies gradually warmed, the haze lifted and visibility returned. We could see for miles. We looked for our roving friends from the previous night. Eventually we caught sight of the men in the distance, with a train of large animals in tow.

They'd found their seventeen lost camels and were headed home.

There was a sense of deep spirituality in that moment. And one of community, too. Even in the absence of external rituals that involved fire, blood, dancing mobs, or drumming circles, we'd just experienced tribalism at its most authentic and profound, internal and real. We had opened our tents and let down our walls for other human beings who needed our help, and it felt right, good, elemental.

In the act of getting beyond ourselves, we became our best selves.

Not everybody has the opportunity to break bread with nomads in an exotic tribal land like Mongolia or celebrate with other Jewish pilgrims at the foot of Mount Meron. And many of us don't belong to synagogues, or haven't yet found one in which we feel comfortable. It doesn't matter—we can still follow the examples of Abraham and Sarah. We can still open our homes and our hearts and strive to become the kinds of Jews that our religious tradition urges us to be.

So what can we do on our own? How do we get beyond ourselves in America's (usually) urban, isolating context?

One option is to get involved with one of the large and growing number of great Jewish community action and social justice organizations out there in need of volunteers, advocates, and supporters (several of them are listed in the back of this book). Some focus their efforts on work in our inner cities, while some send activists abroad to help with projects in developing nations. Others direct their energy toward different areas, such as public policy, education, and politics.

If you'd rather experience something closer to your literal home, you have an opportunity to open your metaphorical tent each and every Friday night. Try to usher in the Jewish Sabbath not just by lighting candles, but by inviting others to join you in your home for a festive meal. They can be friends, neighbors, even acquaintances you barely know. That's the whole point—welcoming the stranger through the biblical value of hospitality. And you can do it with other holidays as well: Share the joy of illuminating the Chanukah menorah, or the mythic power of a Passover Seder, with others. That's how we fuse spirituality and community. That's how we connect with our tribal roots.

Or go a step further: Create your own *havurah*. That might seem like a lot to experiment with, but imagine meeting regularly with an intimate circle of friends, old and new, to discuss books or current events, to study your shared religious heritage, to attend film screenings or visit museums, maybe even to worship together. Just don't be *too* tribal (in the bad sense)—don't be exclusive and exclusionary. That's territorialism, and it almost always results in alienation, resentment, pain, or harm.

And at those times when community isn't enough, when you need to let out some primal steam through a more cathartic, primitive form of emotional expression, construct your own tribalistic ritual.

You don't need to go to Nevada or the Galilee, and you certainly don't need to put up with vendors trying to hawk spiritual tchotchkes. On Lag B'Omer, gather a group of friends and drive to a nearby park or beach. Load up the trunk with logs and kerosene for the bonfire; bring some drums or a portable CD player to help set the appropriate mood; bring a grill and hamburgers (or tofu burgers for the vegetarians) for the celebratory feast. Voilà! Now you have all the ingredients you'll need to create your personalized Lag B'Omer ceremony and dance into the night. . . .

When it works, tribalism breaks down the barriers that separate people from one another. In this technological age, when so many of us feel estranged, detached, and guarded, it has never been more necessary. Reconnecting with our most basic selves will allow us to reconnect with other human beings. But in genuine tribalism, the external rituals must serve internal, core values—values such as interdependence, compassion, commitment, generosity, and spiritual largesse.

Hierarchy matters.

Historically, some of the most creative and influential ideas for revitalizing Jewish life have often flowed from the bottom up, from those on the periphery rather than from insiders. Modern tribalism might not be mainstream, and it might not be associated with an identifiable Jewish movement, but it is a force that must be reckoned with and a raw, rowdy, barrel-chested reservoir of energy and exuberance that can help us to revitalize the desiccated Judaism of our own day.

CHAPTER 6

Beware of False Prophets

YOU KNOW WE'RE IN SERIOUS TROUBLE when Madonna (sometimes known, when it suits her, as Esther) starts to incorporate sacred Jewish mystical symbols into her stage performances, and the non-Jewish actors Demi Moore and Ashton Kutcher get married in Idaho by a so-called rabbi from the Kabbalah Center in L.A.

Welcome to the strange world of California Kabbalah, where self-help and New Age meet Jewish esoterica.

In this weird and wacky cultural climate, anything seems to go when it comes to spiritual expression. While movie stars like John Travolta, Nicole Kidman, and Tom Cruise favor Scientology, celebrities like Barbra Streisand, Roseanne Barr, even Mick Jagger and Elton John prefer to dabble in Jewish mysticism.

If tribalism offers us the raw and primal, popular mysticism—particularly the version of it filtered through the Kabbalah Center and similar groups—provides us with the warm and fuzzy. And, as is the case with most contemporary systems and strategies that offer magic bullets and focus almost exclusively on the individual, it's the baby boomers who are behind this solipsistic societal phenomenon.

Yet again, it's a case of *me me me.*

But this trend has spread far beyond the borders of California. Perhaps in reaction to the dry and ossified Judaism that we see so pervasively around us, the Jewish faith today sometimes seems intoxicated with mysticism.

If that's the situation, what are some of the warning signs that you've encountered a snake-oil salesman rather than the genuine article?

Here are some general guidelines that you might want to carry in your pocket or purse: Stay away from organizations that use the word "Kabbalah" as a marketing tool; watch out for bearded, beady-eyed teachers who wear flowing white robes and red strings around their wrists; beware of those who peddle twenty-five-dollar (and up) vials of specially blessed "holy water" or require that you purchase expensive sets of their self-published books or CDs in order to become one of their disciples.

If you're shopping around for God these days, do your absolute damnedest to keep in mind two important Latin words: caveat emptor.

Our generation's yearning for spiritual sustenance, rooted in some degree of Jewish authenticity, can draw us in to some pretty shady enterprises and drive us toward some fairly unsavory characters. But we can—and should—learn from our mistakes, especially since the commercialization of religion and the phenomenon of charlatanism are nothing new.

Far from it. Even in antiquity the Jewish community faced its own false prophets. The problem was so prevalent in ancient Israelite society that pretenders to the holy office of

Prophet (*Navi* in Hebrew, which translates most accurately as "Seer" or "Visionary") were considered heinous criminals who warranted, and at times received, capital punishment.

In the Bible there are two basic types of prophetic figures: those who were healers and miracle workers (like Elijah, Elisha, and Samuel), and those who functioned as the moral voices of their societies (like Amos, Hosea, and Isaiah). Some were charismatic, some weren't; some were itinerant, some were sedentary; some belonged to officially sanctioned guilds or prophetic communities, some practiced solo.

What united all of them was the fact that they'd been tapped by God for their respective missions, touched by the divine in an unmediated and life-altering way.

It should come as no surprise that the *false* prophets were mirror images of the real ones. The illegitimate prophets of moral indignation were mostly delusional, since there was little status, and no money, to be gained from their self-righteous outbursts. The serious problem was with the so-called healers and miracle workers, polished con artists who made a living from their amulets, incantations, and supernatural cures. These phonies and fakes replaced holiness with hollowness, promising the realization of dreams while emptying the purses of innocent victims.

A false prophet could have good intentions. He might not have been recruited directly by God, but he nevertheless might have wanted to speak with a (fictitious) divine authority in order, for instance, to reform a corrupt society. Yet this approach is still rooted in deception and manipulation, and it is still misguided—as are most strategies that use questionable means to further one's goals.

The Hebrew Bible, a collection of sacred books that spans thousands of years, contains many colorful (and sometimes troubling) illustrations of these kinds of characters. But what was the situation in the post-biblical period? Would the religious establishment of two millennia ago have viewed, say, Jesus of Nazareth—a charismatic, itinerant Jewish teacher and healer—as a false prophet?

You bet your bagels.

In a violent era filled with political and religious turmoil, when dozens of would-be saviors were already roaming the countryside and stirring up even more divisiveness, any person who proclaimed "I am the bread of life: he that comes to me shall never hunger, and he that believes in me shall never thirst" (John 6:35), or who announced "I am the way, the truth, and the life: no man shall come to the Father, but through me" (John 14:6), would have been regarded with deep suspicion. Not only did Jesus claim to have inherited the mantle of prophecy—he claimed to be the Messiah *himself.*

Self-deification is a form of idolatry, and idolatry is one of the most grievous sins you can commit in Judaism. The true Messiah would have ushered in the promised epoch of peace and harmony, love and compassion.

He wouldn't have needed to give it a second shot.

Though some contemporary Bible scholars disagree as to whether the historical Jesus actually identified himself as the Messiah or viewed himself as a divine being, what is beyond dispute is that in the centuries that followed—not even counting the constant, often vicious attacks by the Christian Church and its proselytizers—Jewish communities in the Diaspora were sometimes plagued *internally* by a veritable rogues' gallery of compelling but ultimately destructive false prophets and messiahs. It is a sad and dangerous tradition that has yet to come to a close.

Perhaps the most infamous and influential example is that of Sabbatai Sevi (1626–1676). This young Kabbalist from Smyrna, Turkey, led a messianic movement that swept across the whole Jewish world, from England to Persia, Germany to Morocco, Poland to Yemen. In 1665, while he was living in Gaza in what was then Ottoman Palestine, Sevi declared himself the Messiah. He had already been banished from other cities as a result of his earlier intimations that he was a divine prophet who was above the laws of ordinary human beings. Sevi was excommunicated by Jerusalem's rabbinate, but the Sabbatian movement began to spread far and wide, in large part because of the tireless advocacy and charismatic power of Sevi's chief disciple, Nathan of Gaza.

The Ottoman government eventually imprisoned Sevi in Gallipoli in 1666, where he continued to have visions, preach his mystical theology, and hold court. Stories of miracles began to circulate. Many thousands of Jews, first in Palestine and then in Egypt, Turkey, Europe, and elsewhere, sold their possessions and abandoned their homes in order to pay homage to this mysterious figure. Some were desperate for relief from the poverty and violence that surrounded them. Some wanted to free their souls from the insecurity and fear of belonging to a minority and "alien" people. A pilgrimage that brought them into proximity with the Messiah might achieve those objectives. All that summer, Sevi promised that the world would soon behold spectacular events.

But the Turkish authorities finally had had enough. In September 1666, Sabbatai Sevi was forced to appear before the sultan. He was given a stark, simple choice: Convert to the religion of the empire, or die.

The false messiah became a Muslim.

Sevi's apostasy, his public betrayal of thousands of his followers, plunged much of the Jewish community into despair and disillusionment. It would take generations for them to recover and to regain their footing. Sevi's emergence had sparked a brief and fervent religious revival among Jews all over the globe, yet his ultimate renunciation not only of his messianic role, but of Judaism itself, shattered the lives, the hopes, and, in some cases, the faith of those who believed in him.

Some false prophets are delusional (or mentally ill), some are well-meaning, and some are just grifters who want to make a buck. The bottom line, however, is that no matter what kind of human beings they are, or what their underlying motivation is, their behavior inevitably winds up injuring others.

So why do they continue to attract followers?

Scholars have pointed out that some of the most dramatic outbreaks of messianic movements and false prophets have occurred in the aftermath of tragedy. Sabbatianism, for example, might never have become the phenomenon that it did were it not for the Chmielnicki massacres in Poland and Russia in 1648—massive pogroms that devastated Jewish communities and deflated Jewish spirits, making them desperate (and ripe) for the promise of redemption that a flesh-and-blood Redeemer could provide.

Later pogroms, as well as lingering despair over Sabbatai Sevi's terrible betrayal, gave birth to yet another pretender to the messianic crown, Jacob Frank, a German Jew who lived in the mid-eighteenth century. The charismatic Frank advocated deliberate acts of sin as a means of achieving salvation—he claimed that evil could only be fought with evil. Although he was influenced by Sabbatian thought and its "above the law" theology of religion, Jacob Frank was a much more sinister and nihilistic personality.

But it wasn't only tragedy and trauma that gave rise to imposter prophets and false messiahs.

Over the course of its history, Judaism has gone through turbulent periods in which the general Jewish population has reacted against its religious elite for promulgating a faith tradition that is inaccessible, irrelevant to its needs, or too cerebral. One significant and long-lasting illustration of this trend is the emergence of classical Kabbalah in twelfth-century Spain, a mystical revolt against medieval scholasticism (embodied by rationalist thinkers such as Moses Maimonides).

When a community's ravenous hunger for spirituality is stirred together with social volatility and political instability, the result can be a powerful eruption of messianic mysticism—a petri dish for false prophets.

There are modern manifestations of this phenomenon. Many Jews still live in the dark shadow of the Holocaust, with all its epic tragedy and trauma. Combine the fact of that cataclysm with the social and political upheavals that have been with us since the sixties, the violence and terrorism that roil our world, and the yearning for a spirituality that mainstream Judaism hasn't been able to provide, and you could have predicted that messianic and mystical groups would start to surface in our own time: Jews for Jesus, Messianic Judaism, the Kabbalah Center, Chabad-Lubavitch.

Despite their false promises and inherent deceptions, there have been some surprisingly positive effects that have resulted, sometimes inadvertently, from these groups' occasionally sordid activities. A valuable benefit of popular mysticism—if we can strip it from its dangerous but all too common messianic overlay—is its ability to reach Jews on the margins, those who are disconnected or alienated from organized Judaism and would never walk into one of its institutions; it can feed hungry souls; and it can provoke the religious establishment into reexamining itself.

The status quo, by definition, likes to sit on its ass. It needs to be pushed constantly—and sometimes aggressively—if it is ever to change. That's why, over the centuries, it's often been

only in *reaction* to the misbehavior of rogue figures and movements that mainstream Judaism has reshaped and revitalized
itself.

Well, ladies and gentlemen, the rogues are back—and it's
high time that we do it again.

How do we transform Judaism today? By bucking the prevail-
ing trends of our culture and seeking out the true anchors of
our great faith. While mystical and other esoteric approaches
to Jewish spirituality are compelling and important, what is
much more important is to first have a solid background in the
fundamentals (e.g., the Hebrew language, Jewish holidays and
practices, Bible stories, and the like).

Look at other disciplines: Pablo Picasso learned how to
draw conventional human figures long before his bold experiment with Cubism; Miles Davis trained in classical music
prior to his daring journey into revolutionary forms of jazz.

You don't have to give up on gonzo. In fact, the most rebel-
lious and radical of free spirits are almost always well-rooted
ones—at least until they're ready to soar.

To give a personal example from a different discipline, I've
studied martial arts for more than a dozen years, and it is only
because I have a strong foundation, a black belt in karate, that
I now feel free to experiment with other styles and techniques,
from tae kwon do to boxing. You won't be able to perform
back flips—or commune with God—until you begin by learning how to stand, kick, punch . . . or pray.

In an era when so many of us want quick fixes, this isn't an
easy task—but it's the right one.

The late *New Yorker* writer A. J. Liebling famously referred to boxing as "the sweet science." Like baseball, golf, ten-
nis, and other sports, boxing is related to the principles of
physics. Having a solid foundation at the moment of impact,

using one's body with the right balance of contraction and expansion, minimizing wasted motion and energy, breathing properly and efficiently—all these help to achieve victory in the ring. And all of them take years and years to develop.

When I earned my black belt in karate just after rabbinic ordination, I'd learned not only a particular set of fighting skills, but a surprisingly wide array of other tools and lessons that would help me in my vocation as a religious teacher and counselor: humility, discipline, the power of repetition and practice, empathy, patience, knowing how to channel my abilities constructively, commitment.

Karate helped teach me how to be a teacher. More important, though, it taught me how to be a student.

Most of us aren't boxers or black belts. Yet if, as Jung argued, within each and every human being is a shadow we must confront and contend with, then in a sense we are *all* engaged in psychic combat on a daily basis—and the prize isn't a title or a belt, but a well-balanced soul. To triumph in that invisible, inner arena we need to learn patience, commitment, and humility, among other virtues.

Modernity's shadow is its inability to tolerate this hard-to-swallow reality. Our culture seems much more comfortable declaring:

- *I want it, and I want it now.*

- *I don't have to work for it—I'll just buy this hot new self-help book from a guru I saw on* Oprah *and read it over the weekend.*

- *Nothing is beyond my reach.*

Well, like it or not, some things *are* beyond our reach—in the beginning. When we look for magic bullets, when we skip difficult but crucial steps in our development, we are doing ourselves a terrible disservice. Whether it's in the field of sports, dieting, or finding a more meaningful Judaism, we have to cultivate the virtues above if we're to experience anything in its deepest and most powerful form.

There is absolutely no way to fully understand or appreciate the beauty and majesty of Kabbalah, for example, unless we first have a basic knowledge of Judaism—the foundation from which Kabbalah, and all of Jewish mysticism, emerges. When a group like the Kabbalah Center skips that step (and hence signs up more hungry, impatient, and free-spending students), it can do more harm than good.

It's like when a karate instructor awards a person a black belt too early in their training. That person might swagger down the street with a newfound feeling of strength, but all the teacher has done is given that person a false sense of security, leaving him or her dangerously unprepared in the event of a real-life encounter.

When we're made to think that we know more than we really do, we enter a dream world, a world of shadows rather than substance.

So here's a somewhat impromptu, unsystematic litmus test for the overeager Jewish soul. Before you begin your fast-track classes in mystical exotica and spend a fortune on books, CDs, holy water, and red strings, try to answer a few of the following nuts-and-bolts questions about your religious tradition:

1. Can you name the five books that make up the Torah, Judaism's most sacred and important document?

2. Who were our people's three patriarchs and four matriarchs?

3. Can you list the Ten Commandments?

4. What is the difference between the ancient Temple and the synagogue? Between a biblical priest and a rabbi?

5. What is a mitzvah? Give an example of an ethical and a ritual one.

6. What is Shabbat and why is it considered so important?

7. Compare and contrast Rosh Hashanah and Yom Kippur. How are they connected during the High Holy Day period?

8. What is *kashrut*? Why should we care about the dietary laws today?

9. Identify the major Jewish denominations. What are some of the core ideas and approaches to Jewish life that separate them?

10. Does Judaism believe that life ends with our physical death, or does it believe in a world to come in which our soul lives on?

If these questions—which are, in my view, some of the key building blocks of Jewish literacy—are overly difficult for you, or if they seem completely Greek, then any attempt to delve into the metaphysical mysteries of a subject like the Kabbalah is, at best, premature, and any teacher who would encourage you to explore your spiritual heritage in this kind of reverse order is grossly irresponsible.

And I'm being polite.

The psychologist Abraham Maslow claimed that human be-ings have a hierarchy of needs, an ascending "ladder" from the most basic (food, sleep, sex) to the most advanced (love, wisdom, fulfillment) that we must follow in a logical progression if we're to work our way to the top rung of self-actualization. But I think there is also a hierarchy of knowledge, including religious knowledge. Who'd want to be treated by a cardiologist who'd never taken Biology 101 as an undergraduate? And who'd look to a rabbi for spiritual guidance who knew all about mysticism but who couldn't instruct us about the Bible, conduct a worship service, or console a mourner?

This progression idea applies to us as learners, too.

All we do when we ignore or sidestep the fundamentals is construct a house of cards—something without a true foundation and sound only in appearance. It might look pretty, but even a gentle breeze would collapse the entire structure.

How do we learn the basics? The first and perhaps most difficult step is to admit our ignorance.

Humility, like honesty, is a virtue, but it is a virtue that will give us the strength and fortitude to begin the hard work that is involved in the acquisition of real Jewish knowledge. Once we've humbled ourselves and conceded that we simply can't go it alone if we truly want to explore our faith, the next logical step is to seek out the help of others. The ancient guidebook *Pirke Avot* (*The Sayings of Our Ancestors*) offers two important lessons on this subject: "Do not separate yourself from the community," and "Find yourself a teacher."

For many of us it is the first teaching—connecting with the organized Jewish community—that is the most problematic. Beyond the fact that a lot of us grew up in congregations and communities we didn't like, we have also been raised in a highly individualistic culture, a culture that tells us we don't need to rely on anybody or anything for our own growth. (Jack London, Jack Kerouac, Amelia Earhart—you get the idea.) Solitude can be seductive; trust me, as a rabbi who has served a congregation that at times has been very demanding of me and of my time and space, I know the temptation to flee or withdraw all too well. Yet what takes the real strength, and what is ultimately more enriching, is our interaction with other human beings.

So before we embark on a grand voyage into Jewish mysticism, let's first get over our baggage about joining a group made up of fellow Jews.

There are countless synagogues, federation branches, and JCCs all across the country that offer Introduction to Judaism courses. Look around your own city and sign up for one that suits your schedule and needs. These in-depth courses, which usually run over three or four months, often have a higher percentage of conversion students than inquisitive Jews who simply want to know more about their religion. So what? If you really want to get a firm grounding in Judaism you should jump at the opportunity to study with other seekers and learn, together, about Jewish texts, holidays, ritual observance, philosophy, history, and Hebrew. If you're serious about your spiritual exploration, you've got to do what you'd do in any other endeavor.

You've got to pay your dues—figuratively and literally.

There can be some valuable side benefits, in addition to cultivating Jewish literacy, that are often associated with taking an intro course. One aspect of following the directive not to separate ourselves from the Jewish community is social rather than pedagogic in nature. Whenever a group of people who have common interests or passions gather to discuss them, relationships develop. It's just inevitable. Sometimes those relationships become friendships (whether between singles or couples), and sometimes they evolve into something even more intimate. With a subject as intense and deep as religion, interpersonal relationships can grow equally intense.

Having taught Intro to Judaism courses myself, I've seen this phenomenon with my own eyes: Two women who come from similar backgrounds begin to hang out regularly; a student starts to date someone else in the class—the pair might get serious, even engaged; a different couple decides to host a dinner party for the others in their study group; suddenly, a whole new circle of friends emerges from what was initially a random collection of complete strangers. These shared expeditions into the Jewish tradition frequently result in the unintentional formation of a *havurah,* the tightly knit, mutually supportive group we examined in the last chapter.

Lo and behold, you're now officially part of an "organized" Jewish community—*and it doesn't hurt!*

That's step one. Yet what about the second directive, the one about finding yourself a teacher? Now that you're no longer alone and floundering in the dark, but exploring your faith in the companionship of others, that task becomes much easier. When the introductory class ends, if you want to move to the next level of your studies and build on your Jewish foundation, continue the teacher–student relationship you had with your instructor, usually a rabbi. Or ask around, network with others. All rabbis have different styles and strengths (or weaknesses)— find the rabbinic mentor who is the most appropriate for your interests and the most receptive to your needs.

Rabbis have always been our community's primary educators of Judaism, but you can find a Jewish teacher in other ways. Depending on your particular situation and stage, maybe what you need isn't a rabbi, but a peer, a fellow learner. In classical Jewish education, a *hevruta* is your pedagogic partner, the person with whom you study, discuss, and debate Jewish texts and ideas. Your *hevruta* is the person you learn from as well as the person you teach, the companion on whom much of your religious knowledge—and, I would argue, your spiritual life—in large measure depends.

A *hevruta* (which comes from the same Hebrew root letters as *havurah*) is like an army buddy, and the two of you are engaged, consciously or not, in trench warfare against two adversaries: Jewish illiteracy and a narcissistic culture. Religious education isn't like its secular counterpart; you don't just sit down in an armchair and read on your own. You dialogue, you argue, you interact, you wrestle—and none of these things are possible in a vacuum of the self. With a *hevruta* approach, the roles of teacher and student are in a state of perpetual flux.

Our tradition states that God is present whenever two people study Torah together. Learning, for us, is more than the acquisition of data.

It is a sacrament, a transcendent and profoundly spiritual act.

After you've connected with a community and found a teacher, your Jewish journey has just begun. If this were karate, consider yourself a yellow belt. But now the fun really begins. You have a rock-solid foundation in your faith, you're secure, and you're ready. Unlike those looking to avoid the hard but essential work, you get it. You understand that anything of value in this world, including personal growth and spirituality, involves humility, patience, and discipline. You see that it is the *process,* not necessarily the outcome, that is of paramount import.

And you fully fathom the words from the *Sh'ma* prayer, Judaism's quintessential expression of monotheism: "Take to heart these instructions with which I charge you this day. Impress them upon your children. Recite them when you stay at home and when you are away, when you lie down and when you rise up" (Deuteronomy 6:6–7). It is only through regular, daily study and practice that we can ever hope to realize our goal of developing a literate, revitalized, and truly transformed Jewish soul.

In Judaism, learning for its own sake (*lishma*) is a religious duty and a spiritual virtue. We're judged not by the quantity of our knowledge, but by the quality of our commitment. Still, how seriously we take our study *is* a reflection of that commitment. Consistent Jewish study provides us with the religious knowledge requisite to living a rich and rewarding Jewish life, even as it deepens our devotion. Further, that same learning will also enable us, depending on our dispositions and receptivity, to open new doors to the divine.

Communion follows commitment.

So link with other students and seekers. Take courses in Judaism. Learn the fundamentals of your faith. And, for God's sake, read, read, read. Struggle with your sacred texts on an everyday basis, debate them with a study partner or a friend. (There is a recommended reading list in the back of this book.)

Let your gonzo soul take root before it takes flight—you'll fly higher, you'll soar farther, and your aim will be truer.

And what of today's false prophets and messianic types, the spiritual hucksters and snake-oil salesmen who'd have you believe that a foundation in the basics is unnecessary, who'd toss you recklessly into a mystical ring of fire without having done any of the prep work beforehand, showering you with promises of renewal and redemption? Would a prizefighter trust a trainer who'd be willing to stick him into a ring without good, solid coaching, all in a selfish attempt to earn a quick buck?

The most brazen illustration of the spiritual quick fix can be found in many Pentecostal communities, or in other religious groups that have been influenced by that charismatic stream within Christianity. Pentecostalism promises you instant salvation—once you have made a profession of faith that Jesus is the Messiah and your personal savior. In a culture of religious consumerism, where so many of us pick and choose elements from different religions in order to create our own, customized spiritual path, charismatic Christianity offers you one-stop shopping.

Jews for Jesus, as well as Messianic Jewish congregations, have adopted the Pentecostal model—but with a twist. These groups want to save your soul very badly, and they claim to offer you the best of both worlds, a win-win scenario that you'd be a fool to pass up. In their belief system, you can remain a Jew and retain whatever Jewish practices you follow. All you have to do is accept Jesus as the Messiah. Then, and only then, will you find the fullest expression of your Jewish identity.

You'll also gain what other Jews will never possess: instantaneous salvation, redemption from hell. No fuss, no muss, no sacrifice, just a one-time pledge that will mystically guarantee you peace of mind and eternal life.

Tempted?

I'd sure be, if I didn't know to what extent their theological vision was a mangled distortion of Judaism (thanks to my studies in the fundamentals of the Jewish religion!) and how self-serving and duplicitous their proselytizing actually is.

Let these weirdos come after us. We have nothing to fear but our own ignorance.

Though the Kabbalah Center (now with branches all over the world) doesn't make spiritual redemption seem quite as quick and easy, it's a dangerous entity in its own right. Rabbi Philip Berg and his son, Rabbi Yehuda Berg, have developed a popular messianic-mystical learning system that has become wildly successful, at least in terms of how many participants it has enrolled, how much money it has made, and how much public exposure it's been able to generate. But it is, at its heart, a system of seduction, of shortcuts, of skipping Judaism's building blocks in order to further entice confused and searching Jews with sexier—and more self-oriented—ideas and programs.

Who cares about the Torah or the Talmud when, as the Kabbalah Center instructors claim, all you need to do in order to feel God's presence is to brush your fingers over a page of incomprehensible Hebrew letters?

Who needs to bother with learning about the Ten Commandments when by simply gazing at the seventy-two Kabbalistic names of God you'll release ancient and powerful "energy fields" that will recharge and revitalize your life?

The center's focus on the supernatural rather than the spiritual, on magic rather than real mysticism, is deeply disturbing.

What's the difference between magic and mysticism? Magic is the attempt to manipulate the metaphysical world for personal gain, while mysticism is our attempt to unify *with* it. Genuine Jewish mystics—not today's self-proclaimed Kabbalists—strive to experience God for the sake of the experience itself, not as a means of realizing some sort of benefit, like love, professional achievement, or health. Yet the Kabbalah Center, through its courses and conferences, treats God like a cosmic Pez dispenser, mechanically bestowing (or withholding) existential goodies based on our behavior. We're taught that if we buy and wear their special red strings we'll be protected from the evil eye; if we purchase their multiple-volume set of the Zohar (even if we just let the books sit unopened on our shelves), we'll elevate our souls to unimaginable levels.

Guaranteed.

So how is the Kabbalah Center messianic? Charismatic groups and movements are often driven by charismatic figures. But when respect for a group's leader mutates into the worship *of* that leader, you know a line's been crossed. When the pulp science fiction writer L. Ron Hubbard created Scientology, he positioned himself as its Keeper of Secrets, and he made a fortune before he died from those who wanted to learn those secrets through his books and seminars. Charisma is not an indicator of character. Some of the most magnetic and compelling personalities can also be some of the slickest and most unethical. It's one thing to be a teacher and guide. It is another to present yourself as a divinely appointed guru, the holy conduit through which all must pass in order to gain access to teachings and practices that will renew or redeem our lives.

If that's not playing the role of a messiah, I don't know what is.

The Berg family has followed a similar, troubling path. Like Scientology, the Kabbalah Center gives special attention and treatment to celebrities while exploiting ordinary people. Like L. Ron Hubbard once did, the Berg family has enriched itself at the expense of unknowing, often needy student victims—and simultaneously elevated their own status as master Kabbalists with spiritual gifts who have inherited mystical secrets known only to them, but that are given out, gradually, for a fee. The Kabbalah Center and its founders have been widely denounced by top Jewish scholars and established rabbinical associations, not because Kabbalah itself is a problem, but because it is presented by the center in a way that warps its meaning and purpose, and, in the process, commercializes and trivializes one of Judaism's richest traditions.

As a longtime student and lover of authentic Jewish mysticism in its many and varied forms, I say let's condemn the Kabbalah Center for what it is—a cult of personality and a crass, money-grubbing sham.

Okay, and now I'll tell you how I *really* feel. . . .

———

Biblical prophets often fought for the rights of individuals to make their own religious and moral decisions, free of oppression or coercion; they didn't *make* those decisions for others, which is what occurs so frequently in modern-day cults led by spiritual charlatans, self-appointed prophets, and messianic pretenders. While there is much to admire about the Chabad-Lubavitch movement (as I discussed in the fourth chapter), the way it treated, and continues to treat, its last rebbe, Menachem Mendel Schneerson, definitely isn't one of them.

While the first Lubavitcher Rebbe was one of the most important leaders in the early years of Hasidism (which, like the Kabbalah, is itself a dynamic and beautiful mystical movement), he never held himself up as a messianic figure, nor was he viewed as one by his disciples. That changed two centuries later, when Schneerson, the seventh Lubavitcher Rebbe, became the group's leader.

Chabad members, as well as many other Jews, sought the guidance and blessing of this brilliant, charismatic personality. People would come to his residence in Crown Heights, Brooklyn, from all over the world and wait in long lines for hours to have their personal audience—usually consisting of just a few seconds—with this great holy man. The Rebbe would bless babies and marriages and offer prayers for those with illnesses. But he went further. He'd tell people who they should or shouldn't marry, or which job they should accept or leave. He made decisions for people, and people allowed him to take away their autonomy. Why? Because of the messianic aura that had grown around Schneerson, an aura he allowed to exist. As far as I'm aware, the Rebbe never said anything publicly to discourage the way he was being viewed and treated, and he never took himself out of the role of supernatural guru to the Jewish masses.

I attended a crowded afternoon service one day in Crown Heights, a service during which Schneerson, unable to walk or speak because of a stroke, made one of his final public appearances. (He died a few months later.) Standing in the packed sanctuary, I heard the following chant, a chant that reverberated throughout the room: "May our master, our teacher, and our rabbi, *King Messiah,* live forever!" Then, in the midst of the ecstatic, mantralike chanting, Schneerson's assistants drew back a red velvet curtain to reveal the Rebbe/King Messiah, seated on a large chair, to the assembled multitude. The chanting intensified in a frenzy of emotion. After several seconds the curtain was drawn closed again. It was like something out of *The Wizard of Oz.*

To say I was distressed by the experience is an understatement. This wasn't respect for a leader—it was worship of an idol.

Even now, years after the Rebbe's death, there are actually fax machines next to Schneerson's tomb in a cemetery in Queens. Their purpose? To receive transmissions from followers of "King Messiah," petitions for prayers and blessings, requests for advice about personal or professional matters, confessions of sins. It would be comical if it weren't for the fact that people really believe that the Rebbe will continue to help them and tell them what to do—from beyond the grave.

Here again we see yet another illustration of people looking to take the easy path, to skip steps, to find shortcuts to heaven. The motivation for Schneerson's interventions might have been laudable. But having an intercessor between human beings and God—even if that were possible—relieves us of the burden of doing the heavy lifting, the hard work that is so essential to our religious and spiritual development. The good news is that in Judaism we don't *need* intercessors and intermediaries to have a relationship with God. We just need to take responsibility for our lives, including our Jewish lives, and act with the commitment and humility that is warranted.

Gurus, rebbes, prophets, messiahs—the panoply of spiritual offices and personalities can be bewildering, and at times frightening. Who's a phony and who's for real? Who wants to share his or her wisdom with us, and who wants our money or our souls? In the face of this complexity and uncertainty, the best we can do is hold firm in our faith, pursue lifelong study and engagement with both it and our community, and remain vigilant. Today's Jews, particularly in the West, have largely escaped the violence and material impoverishment that plagued previous generations, the sense of hopelessness and desperation that served as triggers for eruptions of sometimes very destructive religious charlatanism and chicanery.

But ours is an age of *spiritual* impoverishment, and those who would feed on our fears are still around. They know we're wounded. They smell blood.

Yet despite all the problems and our need to be wary, one positive aspect of this renewed interest in the mystical is that, as it did in the past, it is stirring up the pot. Like the populist (and at times questionable) mystics and holy men and women of prior eras, some of the contemporary mystical teachers and groups are reaching Jews on the margins, those who are disconnected or alienated from Judaism and wouldn't even contemplate entering a mainstream Jewish institution. They are provoking the religious establishment into reexamining itself. They are exposing the uninitiated to a deep spiritual stream within our ancient tradition, even though they too frequently present it prematurely and simplified, or in radically distorted form.

If we can get people to take a first step through the door to their Judaism, and if mysticism "lite" is one way to do it, then some of these groups have a part to play—as long as we keep them on a very tight leash, and educate those who are disaffected but intrigued about the dangers they're likely to confront. It's not an ideal situation, but it's the one we've been handed.

Just as his military superiors told Martin Sheen's character in *Apocalypse Now* to proceed with great caution when he entered the jungle, on the way to his rendezvous with Colonel Kurtz, I'd say the same thing to any of you who asked me how to navigate the wilderness of modern mysticism. And if you do encounter some of these ambiguous and at times shady characters on your journey, use the same "extreme prejudice" that Sheen was advised to use in your dealings with them.

You could learn a lot—about yourself as well as them.

CHAPTER 7

The Road from Wine and Roses to Shock and Awe

THE MOST IMPORTANT SEASON in the Jewish calendar is the *Yomim Noraim,* almost always translated as the vague but pleasant-sounding High Holidays. Not only is this a lousy English translation, it's a metaphor for the way we've neutered and neutralized Judaism's elemental power. What the Hebrew phrase actually means is Days of *Awe,* an intensive ten-day period of introspection, contrition, and spiritual transcendence. What ought to be potent and strong has become light and sweet. Even worse, in our current laissez-faire condition, our comfort food has grown foul with banality.

But we don't need to be treated with kid gloves—we need to be agitated. Our generation calls for a Judaism that is bold, confrontational, and smack in your face.

We want to be pushed. And we want to push back.

Artists, perhaps more than any other group, seem to understand our emotional and spiritual need to be challenged, to be placed, on occasion, in a zone of discomfort in order to grow in our minds, hearts, and souls. Artists are usually eager to question assumptions, rebel against conventions, and provoke the status quo. They're itching to stir up society and the way society views itself and the world—often with the goal of using their imagination to produce personal or social transformation. Look at the tactics of guerilla or street theater, abstract expressionism, surrealism, minimalism.

Modern artists have generally been hostile toward organized religion. I find that fact unfortunate and ironic, since I believe the border between inspiration and revelation is extremely porous. Both of these phenomena, whether they occur on the aesthetic or the spiritual plane, are connected to an exceptional, powerful, incomprehensible kind of *disclosure*. That's why I also think that artists, musicians, and poets are often better equipped than religionists to fathom and more fully express the mystery and life-altering might of Transcendence—what a guy like me would call God.

That historic hostility toward religion is starting to give way to a new openness. A growing number of Jews in the arts today have not only begun to express their Jewishness in fresh, daring, and provocative ways—some have actually found (or in some cases rediscovered) their religious identities through their creative work.

In the case of Marc Maron—stand-up comic, writer, and performance artist—hostility has taken on new meaning and become a hallmark of his Jewish identity as well as his craft. Although he was born in New Jersey, Maron grew up in Albuquerque, New Mexico, and had lived in Anchorage, Alaska, prior to that. "My parents," he recounts, "were the first generation of Jews to move as far away from their parents as possible for reasons other than fleeing the country."

In Albuquerque, Maron's family did belong to a temple, and

Marc attended Hebrew school there. "I became a terror," says Maron. "I saw no reason to go to religious school other than to make the teachers cry. I didn't take it seriously. My engagement with my Jewishness was cultural, not religious. My heroes were Jewish comics like Lenny Bruce, Jewish baseball players, even Jewish gangsters. I've always considered myself a spiritual person, but that world didn't offer me a pathway to God."

Maron started his comedy career in the late eighties in Los Angeles. Since then, he has appeared in countless clubs across the nation and is a regular guest on the television talk show circuit, particularly the *Late Show with David Letterman* and *Late Night with Conan O'Brien,* where I first witnessed his acerbic wit and incisive cultural and political commentary.

On his Web site Maron refers to himself as "self-loathing, neurotic, and angry." When I ask him if any of those attributes relate to the Jewish aspect of his identity, Maron explains: "It took years to accept myself as a caricature. I was brought up on Woody Allen films—that was my context for someone who is Jewish, and gradually I gravitated to that middle-class Jewish image. To this day, I am not happy or satisfied with myself— but I think that is a *Jewish* phenomenon. You've got to always be driving forward, riling people up, never feeling that you're ever good enough. I think Jewishness is expressed through restlessness itself."

Maron is known by many as a Jewish comedian. But what does that mean? "For a long time," Maron recollects, "I didn't talk about being Jewish without fear of being hackneyed. I didn't want to be associated with all that Borscht Belt bullshit—I wanted to express myself, and my anger, in a shameless way. I was talking about masturbating and other things directly and personally. I wanted to transcend my fear of embarrassment. I had some trouble with my career early on because of that. But for me, comedy is rooted in—I don't

know what the hell else to call it—in the almost religious revelation that you're fucked, I'm fucked, and very few of us have
the courage to face this shit. That, to me, is Jewishness. It's social and cultural criticism, it's the prophetic voice, but it's also
the voice of the clown."

And how is a prophet like a clown?

"I've learned that you have to let people laugh *at* you if
you're to get this tough message across. I've always thought
that people had the same existential pain and fears if they'd
just let themselves feel them. So in my act I try to slip that message in and make people realize that they're not alone. I'm a
stand-in for everybody else in the room, a surrogate, a circus
clown. I wasn't comfortable with that role at first. But when
the whole thing works, there's a rush of revelation and identification. Our ancestors must have laughed their asses off at the
prophets, but look at what those guys did, look how they irri-
tated and pushed their societies to be better."

Maron is perhaps best known for his one-man show
Jerusalem Syndrome (which was later made into a book). The
Jerusalem Syndrome is a genuine psychological phenomenon
that can strike visitors to the Holy Land and make them believe that they've suddenly been given special wisdom or become vessels for the divine voice. The show traces Maron's
own spiritual journey and lifelong quest for meaning and purpose. It includes observations from his own trip to Israel.

"I've always asked myself," Maron says, "why do I feel special? There are a lot of models for explaining human beings.
In the show I used a religious, as opposed to a psychological,
model. If only people knew the secret knowledge I knew, we'd
all be better. So was that God talking to me? Or a demon?
Was I delusional or on track? In my late twenties and early
thirties, I felt I was being personally led by a mystical power.
I'm sure the coke and other drugs had some effect on my self-

perception. But even when I went to Israel, I felt that power. I became enchanted with the Temple Mount and stories of the Messiah—enchanted in a kind of dark, apocalyptic way."

Maron sees religiosity in both the sacred and the profane. He's fascinated by Orthodox Jews: "With their cryptic texts, zeal, secret handshakes—they're like the Freemasons. We *need* their extremism in order to make us all feel that we're not good enough as Jews." Maron is also fascinated by the commercial products and culture of corporate America, with its omnipresent, mass-market iconography, from the Nike swoosh logo to the famous Coca-Cola signature.

If "religious" symbols and images are all around us, I ask Maron, then why is it such a leap to try the Jewish religion as an adult?

"Because I'm pissed off at my parents," he answers. "What else could it be? The symbols of Judaism haven't been made resonant with me. Who runs synagogues? Who runs Jewish organizations? It's all so political, and I don't give a shit about it. It's alienating and insulating to me. I don't want to be limited by a label or associated with a stereotype—that's why I avoided Jewish comedy for so long. I'd be open to Judaism if I could see how these rituals and teachings and traditions would help me through my existential condition. But I haven't sought it out."

I inform him that there are a lot of new and dynamic things going on in the Jewish world today. I ask him why he hasn't bothered to look.

"I've been prideful. I wanted to be seen as some guy who doesn't need anybody or anything, a rugged individualist, a cowboy, a maverick. I'm not a team player. But as I get older, I see that that self-perception is grounded in my own pride. I *want* that connection to my tradition, I want to have a relationship with God and the joy and the catharsis that comes

with it. But I fight it—I still resent authority of any kind. Yet
I see that this is all part of my pride, my craving for control,
my need to rebel. These themes and struggles come out in my
work, but I've recoiled a bit since *Jerusalem Syndrome,* and I
feel stifled. To be honest, I'm afraid to confront some of this
shit."

There are a large number of disaffected Jews out there who
are afraid, perhaps unconsciously, to confront their disaffection with Judaism—and all that is inevitably associated with
that uncomfortable feeling (like guilt, loneliness, a sense of
confusion or despair). But disaffection is still a sign of *engagement,* still a signal that a person is struggling, sometimes fever-
ishly, with a relationship that matters to them. Based on my
observations of people in my own congregation and around
the country, this "struggling" phenomenon is the rule rather
than the exception. And it may be even more pronounced
among Jews in the fields of art and entertainment.

Though he is only in his thirties, the playwright Daniel
Goldfarb has achieved remarkable success in the theater
world. Goldfarb grew up in Toronto and was raised in a home
with a strong sense of Jewish cultural identity. He went
through the motions of a conventional and solid Jewish up-
bringing (attending Hebrew school, having a bar mitzvah, going to Jewish summer camp, traveling to Israel, sitting
through High Holiday services), but it was the discussions
around the family dinner table, debates about the latest Philip
Roth novel, Woody Allen film, or exhibition of Marc Chagall's
paintings, that fueled his Jewish soul.

"I wouldn't call myself religious," says Goldfarb. "Institutional Judaism never really did it for me. Jewish culture did."

Drama had been Goldfarb's chosen mode of expression
since the age of three or four, when he'd put on shows for his

parents. After they took him to New York to see some larger-scale productions, Goldfarb was hooked on theater. In the twelfth grade he wrote a play called *And the Lord Spoke to Judas,* a play that dealt with God, faith, religion, individualism, community. It was a reflection of the Jewish community in Toronto he knew so well.

"I wasn't consciously writing Jewish plays," he says today, "but Jewish themes and characters just kept emerging in my work."

Goldfarb moved to Manhattan and studied dramatic writing at New York University and then Juilliard. He knew that he wanted to write plays professionally. While an undergrad at NYU, Goldfarb wrote one of his "angriest" plays, a social satire called *Oedipus Jew.* It was about Jewish mothers and their sons, a riff on new Jewish stereotypes, like the insecure guys he knew from home and school who'd pump iron to ward off the image of the weakling Jew and momma's boy. Goldfarb used the classic Greek tragedy as the model for his play, replete with a chorus of overbearing Jewish mothers and an alienated, furious, matricidal son.

"I wrote other plays during that time," Goldfarb says, "plays that weren't written in a Jewish voice. But it just didn't feel right. It didn't sound authentic, like my own, honest voice. You know the cliché, the one that says we should 'write about what you know'? Well, it's true, or at least it was for me."

While an MFA student at Juilliard, Goldfarb wrote the first of his plays to ever be produced (in 1999), *Adam Baum and the Jew Movie.* It's a play about a fictional Jewish movie mogul, a Hollywood film executive with a complicated and some-times self-loathing relationship with his religious identity. He hires a gentile screenwriter to make a new film for the studio, but, ironically, the result feels *too* Jewish to him—he doesn't want to produce what he calls a "Jew movie." All of this transpires around the time of the bar mitzvah of the executive's son. As this important and emotional Jewish rite of passage nears, the identity war that has always been taking place covertly within the mogul's soul now rushes to the surface of his life and consciousness, forcing the man to confront who he really is.

"Plays have to be immediate," Goldfarb claims. "They have to be about need and want and drive. Anger is a great place to start them. My plays have been rooted in my own confusion, in trying to figure out my Jewishness and how it fits into my life. Though I'm not religious, not even particularly spiritual, I am a Jew, and I want to understand what that means—for *me*."

When his play *Modern Orthodox* opened on Broadway in 2004, Goldfarb was finally able to expose his ideas to a wider audience. When he started to write it, Goldfarb thought his play would be a scathing exposé on the hypocrisy of Orthodox Jews, but instead it became a romantic comedy, "a valentine to modern Orthodoxy." The play is about what happens when a modern Orthodox diamond merchant—a sort of stand-in for organized Jewish religion—enters the lives of two young, cosmopolitan, largely secular Jews who live together but are reluctant to marry.

"It is essentially a fable about commitment and faith," says Goldfarb. "What's the connection? This play allowed me—I was still single at the time I wrote it—to explore personal and theological themes I'd been thinking about for a very long time. When this urban, pretty much secular couple struggles with what it would really mean to utter Jewish prayers and recite vows before God, even if you're not into Judaism and don't believe in God, that's me. Or, rather, that *was* me."

Writing plays has become Goldfarb's primary mode of expressing and struggling with his Jewish identity: "In general, I'm not that comfortable with the Jewish community, nor am I very comfortable with the Jewish religion. How do I reconcile all that with where I am today as a contemporary Jew? Theater lets me wrestle with that question, and it's the wrestling part that I find so unique, so extraordinary, so Jewish. That's what links me to Judaism."

As Goldfarb continues his journey of self-expression and self-discovery, he is bringing in others who can relate to his wrestling. His plays are gateways for Jews who feel no link to formal Jewish institutions, but who want the sanctuary of a dark theater in which to ponder their own identities. "My foundation as a Jew is a huge part of who I am," Goldfarb says. "I had no idea that my Jewishness was that important to me until I sat down and started writing. The arts helped reveal to me who I really was, and now they help me to explore who I want to be."

Not every member of this generation of Jews is engaged in some kind of struggle with Judaism. Some Jews are simply looking for new entry points, creative, often artistic ways of reconnecting with their cultural tradition—and it is Jewish culture, not religion, that so clearly seems to be the gateway for a deeper exploration of our faith (and not just for artists). One of the cutting-edge events that attracts Jewish performers and musicians as well as Jews interested in the arts and music is the Knitting Factory's Jewsapalooza festival in downtown Manhattan.

Jewsapalooza was first held in the early nineties as both a showcase for a sometimes radical rereading of Jewish heritage music (such as folk, jazz, and klezmer) and a hip, alternative

destination for young Jews during the Christmas party season.
The multievening festival has been a wild success. It continues
to grow and to serve as an important venue for the celebration
and affirmation of contemporary Jewish culture and life,
though it occurs in a distinctly nontraditional setting.

In fact, since so many of today's Jews are drawn to the arts,
it is frequently in nontraditional, even non-*Jewish* settings that
we are more likely to find them. In 2005, the Brooklyn Academy of Music—a center for avant-garde music, dance, theater,
and cinema—held its first Too Cool for Shul series. While I'd
argue that a shul can be a pretty cool place when it's done right
(and that some of these alternative festivals try a bit too hard to
be hip), BAM's celebration of Jewish culture through a month
of stand-up comedy, musical performances, film, and panel
discussions explored key elements of Jewish expression
through a decidedly unorthodox lens.

And what of the "shock and awe" mentioned in this chapter's title? The shock, in this context, comes from the sight of
hundreds of young Jews embracing and rejoicing in their Jewishness in this largely secular and materialistic day and age,
and the awe is what they might experience internally when
they discover deep resonance with—and inspiration from—a
tradition they'd formerly dismissed out of hand.

That inspiration doesn't spring from sentimentality or nostalgia. These festivals don't include cheesy productions of *Fiddler* or cheery, childish dreidel songs. They are, instead,
celebrations of the *next* wave of Jewish culture, one that is
grounded in the past but unafraid of the future. Young Jewish
artists, musicians, writers, filmmakers, and comics are striving
for self-expression, as have others before them—but they are
doing it on their own terms. Discovery, not dogma, is their
guide.

This new, gonzo Jewish wave is about exploration and provocation.

It is Judaism unbound.

Melissa Shiff is a young installation artist. Like so many other men and women of her generation, Shiff was raised by her parents as a secular Jew. "But I had a strong sense that I was Jewish," she says. "Though we weren't conventionally observant, one of the things that was transmitted to me about the Jewish tradition was that Judaism is about social justice and social action. In my adult life I consider myself postdenominational, and I continue to identify with Judaism through my pursuit of social justice. As an artist I do that by creating rituals that speak to these issues."

Shiff studied at the School of the Museum of Fine Arts in Boston. After her graduation in 2001, she moved to Manhattan. It was there that she staged her first public art/social action Jewish ritual performance, *Times Square Seder: Featuring the Matzo Ball Soup Kitchen.* One of the video sculptures Shiff made for this creative and ritual "happening" was acquired by the Jewish Museum for their permanent collection.

Artistic expression and ritual enactment are complementary elements in Shiff's work. "When I was studying at the Museum School," she recalls, "I learned about many different art forms, and I employ two of them in my own practice. One of these is conceptual art, which generally eschews the art 'object,' while the other is installation art, which is about creating architectural environments with multimedia. I've found a way to combine these two approaches—which to some people seem mutually exclusive—by means of the Jewish rituals that I reinvent and reformat."

Judaism doesn't hinder Shiff as an artist—it helps her to

become the artist she wants to be. It isn't a source of struggle, but of synthesis. Jewish ritual functions as the connective tissue in her work, allowing her to fuse forms, connect with her religious heritage, and even make political statements.

"In my latest installation I built a Passover environment out of four thousand pieces of Manischewitz matzos. I created six hundred pillows and covered the entire floor of the installation with them. All of the pillows had an image of a matzo silk-screened onto them with the words 'Crush Oppression' written on top of the matzo image. Each pillow was stuffed with a piece of matzo, so that when the visitor walked through the installation they were crushing the Bread of Affliction— the bread of oppression. The installation itself was called 'The Medium Is the Matzo.' The matzo became the message. The idea was to get the person who walked through and over my installation to think about the idea and the need to crush today's oppression."

Does her use of Jewish ritual objects make Shiff a religious Jew? I would argue that it does, if we'd only let ourselves be as open and expansive in our interpretation of what it means to be religious as Shiff is through the construction of her installations.

"My Judaism has helped to enhance my art practice and creativity," says Shiff. "Judaism is the fertile ground that I cull to make artwork. It gives me a foundation and frame and history from which to make creative commentary on today's social issues."

Shiff brings up her own, real-life wedding to illustrate her point: "My husband Louis and I created both a traditional Jewish wedding and a performance-art piece. We called it 'Avant-Garde Jewish Wedding.' With this ritual, we wanted to make the point that identity is at once an inheritance and a performance. For our wedding, I used video technology to enhance the ritual. I turned the *chuppah* [marriage canopy] into a movie screen and made nine different video segments that were projected onto it at different times throughout the ceremony. One of the segments was called 'Rewriting Deuteronomy.' It was important for both of us to look into the sexism of Orthodox Jewish marriage and to convey the message that Judaism is open to change and reinterpretation."

She explains her segment choice: "We found a passage in Deuteronomy that said that if a woman's virginity was found not to be intact at the time of marriage, then the men of her village should stone her to death. Obviously, Jewish practice today doesn't embrace such harsh customs. But I wanted to show that the Torah must speak to each generation. That's why we rewrote this sexist passage to find words more suitable for our marriage ceremony."

Rather than rejecting the Jewish wedding tradition out of hand, Shiff "marries" the ritual to her art, and, in the process, discovers the joy in both.

Rethinking and reworking Jewish ritual *is* Shiff's Jewish practice, her way of identifying as a Jew. It's also her path for finding creative ways to link with and learn about the observances and rites of Judaism—and to tap into its rich culture of interpretation, debate, and, at times, protest. By exploring new ways of approaching and reimagining ancient objects and practices, Shiff can affirm and celebrate her faith publicly and proudly, despite those aspects she finds problematic.

She wishes that others of her generation would open up and approach Judaism in a similar fashion, even if they're not artists. "It would be nice if people elaborated on their rituals," Shiff says. "Wouldn't it be wonderful if people were actually brave enough to reinvent their rituals at home and to move beyond viewing them as being simply about the transmission of identity? The Passover ritual in particular has such incredible potential for social action and activism. After all, there is a mandate in the Haggadah that declares, 'Let all who are hungry come in and eat.' So maybe in the future people will actually *enact* this, and change their rituals from stories that are merely told into stories that are acted upon."

Archie Rand, who teaches art at Brooklyn College, is one of the pioneers in the area of interweaving art with Jewish expression. Since the mid-seventies Rand has made hundreds of creative works based on Jewish subjects and themes that derive from both literal and interpretive readings of the Torah, the Talmud, *midrashim* (rabbinic legends), and the Kabbalah. "I believe there are other Jewish artists," says Rand, "who actually feel more of a tie to their Jewishness than they are willing to admit. They are afraid of it. They don't want to be identified with it. I've chosen a different way, and it has given me a great deal in return."

As a youth, Rand attended religious school and Orthodox services, but he is largely self-taught in his spiritual tradition. Still, he is not an observant Jew in the conventional sense, and he rarely goes to synagogue. Despite his nonobservance, Rand insists on the right to boldly proclaim his Jewish identity: "I just came in and invaded it. Why not recorral Jewish identity and Jewish memories?"

Rand exults openly in his Jewishness. He grew up in New York at a time when being Jewish carried fewer burdens, reservations, or embarrassments than it did in the generation of his parents and grandparents, and for that reason—as well as because of his own somewhat raucous personality—Rand's vulnerability as a Jew is far less apparent than that which was often experienced by older artists who lived through the stress of immigration and the years of the Holocaust. His positive attitude about being Jewish, coupled with his fearlessness about expressing it, has made Rand an artist who doesn't feel constrained by Judaism, even as he is grounded in it.

Rand will often juxtapose, without explanation, an extraordinary range of at times incomprehensible and incoherent images and motifs from a wide variety of sources. When he speaks of his art, he frequently uses the same language of revelation, of mystical disclosure, that others in this chapter have conveyed. Speaking on one of his pieces, Rand once said: "I had the feeling that it had not come from me, but through me, that I had been an instrument of God. I think that every good artist who ever lived gets that feeling when he does the work he really has to do."

Rand's words here seem especially relevant for younger artists who identify themselves as mystical or spiritual Jews but who are not closely affiliated with synagogues or communal organizations. Rand, unlike many of today's rejectionists, has the credibility to bypass formal religious institutions and classic rituals precisely because he has such a solid foundation and basic literacy in them.

Rand is an outsider who is also an insider, and his art embodies this paradox.

In some ways Rand is a one-man outreach program for alienated Jews. His goal is as ambitious as it is audacious: to create an entire visual Jewish culture based on different ways of interpreting and visualizing biblical stories, liturgical prayers, and mystical tracts. This kind of approach allows each viewer to apprehend and connect with Rand's work in a diverse and intensely personal fashion.

Rand sometimes sounds more like a missionary than an artist. He says that he wants his creative works to be viewed as aids or windows to prayer "across which meaningful devotions can be mediated toward heaven. One doesn't pray to an image but through it. Art serves to act for the greater glory of God." Rand doesn't do battle with Judaism—he harmonizes it, and in his hands the connection between art and Jewish spirituality becomes palpable. The image, in Rand's eyes, is a portal to the divine, not a substitute for it, or, as it is for secular artists, an end in itself.

Since 1974, Rand has made at least fifteen different sets and series of works that employ Jewish images, some consisting of as many as fifty or more individual panels. At this writing, he is engaged in creating a painting for each of the 613 *mitzvot,* or sacred commandments delineated in the Torah.

In 1981, Rand completed twelve stained-glass windows for Anshe Emet Synagogue in Chicago (one for each biblical tribe of Israel), and the following year he produced three additional windows depicting the patriarchs Abraham, Isaac, and Jacob for Temple Sholom, another Chicago congregation. Both of these projects utilized abstract or representational imagery rather than realistic figures.

By the mid-eighties Rand had begun to reinterpret and express Jewish motifs and mythic narratives in even more idiosyncratic, experimental styles, often combining secular elements with religious ones. In 1989, for example, Rand created "The Chapter Paintings," a set of fifty-four paintings based on the weekly portions of the Torah that are read and reread in synagogues every year. Rand selected a passage from each of the portions that he illustrated in a highly abstract or fantastical manner. Image played off of text (at times incorporating text) to produce a visual narrative of the Torah.

This set the stage for a more direct and irreverent approach to interpreting and celebrating the Jewish tradition. In "Sixty Paintings from the Bible" (1992), Rand illustrated key events from the Hebrew Scriptures in a cartoonlike style, with biblical figures frequently having word-filled balloons extending from their mouths. In the panel based on Genesis 3:7, for instance, the balloon above Adam and Eve, situated in the Garden of Eden, reads: "We're naked." In 2002, Rand reached beyond cartoonlike forms to a comic-book format for "The Nineteen Diaspora Paintings," where his biblical characters, while identified by traditional Hebrew script, are usually dressed in urban clothing styles from the thirties and forties.

On a personal level, Rand found that he could easily relate to a comic-strip format because many of the pioneers in that field were Jews: "I wanted to break from stereotyped Yiddishized nostalgia. So I looked at guys I was looking at as a kid—DC Comics, *Tales from the Crypt*. I did not want to make paintings that were about Jewishness, but paintings that *were* Jewish, and that didn't indulge an unlived, imported nostalgia or invoke a predictable iconography." Through his most recent work Rand has striven to make art that appealed to contemporary Jewish American sensibilities, free of sentimental, Eastern European associations.

But it is not free of Judaism. On the contrary, despite Rand's unorthodox methods and images, the source of his inspiration comes from the Jewish religion itself, with all its holy books, sacred rites, and mystical ideas.

Some of the artists and performers that have been highlighted in this chapter speak about their relationship with Judaism as being marked by struggle, one that plays itself out in their work. Others describe Judaism as a way of achieving synthesis between their craft and their faith, their creativity and their identity. For some it is Jewish culture that is the predominant element they employ (or respond to) in their art; for others it is Jewish ritual or text. The linkages vary greatly from artist to artist, and they are not always neat, clean, and clear. In the realm of music, arguably the most intangible art of them all, these murky lines of interconnection between creative expression and organized religion can often be even more difficult to trace.

But you better believe they are there.

Frank London is a musician and composer who lives in the East Village and who grew up in Plainview, Long Island ("It lives up to its name," he says). London describes his religious background as "typically Jewish suburban"—he attended religious school twice a week through his bar mitzvah, went to services on occasion at his family's synagogue, and celebrated ("a better word would be 'observed,' as Lenny Bruce said") most of the Jewish holidays at home.

"In retrospect," says London, "the Judaism of my youth was a good, healthy, Jew-positive, consistent, nonhypocritical experience. But pieces were missing. I never learned about how other Jews practiced, or about the deeper meanings of *kashrut* and Shabbat, or about Hasidism and ecstatic singing and dancing. The whole thing was presented as a fait accompli: Here it is, folks. There was no mysticism at all, just a sort of spirituality lite. But I was taught a firm, solid, liberal, humanistic worldview that probably shaped my own more than I admit."

A lot of today's Jews talk about their cultural connection to Judaism without ever really defining in concrete terms what culture actually means. That's not the case with London. He chooses his words and definitions very carefully: "Am I a 'cultural' Jew? Ah, there's the rub. Other than the humanism that was imparted to me, where and when I grew up there was no Jewish culture of any interest to me—no ethnicity, no cool Jewish music, no Yiddish language. Food was the only ethnic symbol. My grandfather Lou owned a delicatessen in Brooklyn, and I grew up running errands for him. That felt more real. The music in temple was of no interest to me, nor was the Israeli music danced to at bar mitzvah and wedding parties. No, my culture as a kid was 100 percent American weird rock pop alternative hippie culture."

All that changed dramatically while London was pursuing his passion and studying at the New England Conservatory of Music in Boston. He'd never imagined that Judaism would ever play a role in his musical endeavors—until one instructor exposed London to a domain he didn't know existed:

"The first radical Jewish cultural moment was when I was in college, learning about the world of music, broadening my horizons—heck, it was like Dorothy seeing the world become Technicolor after black-and-white. Salsa, jazz, classical, Haitian, Balkan music—who knew? Into this picture came Ashkenazic, Eastern European Jewish/Yiddish music and culture. I was introduced to this thing called 'klezmer' by a colleague and teacher, Hankus Netsky, who knew about this music from his family. He played us some old recordings and we were, like, 'Cool, this music rocks!' *On its own terms,* coincidental to the fact that it was the Jewish music of my ancestors."

It was London's "shock and awe" moment, his revelatory experience as a Jew and as a musician. He'd discovered something he could connect with on multiple levels, that could inform him, inspire him, shake his soul to its core.

London goes on: "We learned it, played it at a concert, and then one of those accidents of historical imperative took over. It turned out that at that moment in time, in post-*Roots* America, during a period of hyphenated American-ness, Jews were looking for a cultural experience to tie their own identity to— and for a moment, klezmer became their soundtrack. It was contemporary to the more spiritual *havurah* movement as well as the post-Vietnam protest movement, and the klezmer revival tied into both the spiritual and political needs and desires of myself and many American Jews. This was especially true when the Klezmatics came along, rejected nostalgia and kitsch, and made radical Jewish politics, aesthetics, history, and mysticism our credo. We became a major voice in the contemporary klezmer renaissance and in the Jewish revival movement. And all just because we were doing the right thing in the right time and place."

In addition to his role as one of the founders of the Klezmatics, London has been prolific over the years as a musical artist in many areas. He has over twenty of his own recordings and has been on more than a hundred CDs with artists ranging from David Byrne to LL Cool J to the indie-rockers They Might Be Giants. London's most recent CDs are *Hazonos* (with Cantor Jacob Mendelson), which documents his fascination with classic liturgical and cantorial music, and *Carnival Conspiracy* (with London's own Klezmer Brass Allstars and over forty other guest musicians and vocalists, including some of the best Yiddish singers in the world), which is, in London's words, "a nonstop Jewish fiesta, a fusion of frenzied Hasidic pop with Brazilian-Mexican-Yiddish songs of love and angst." London's compositions have been performed at Carnegie Hall, and he has written scores for dance and film. He still plays trumpet and other instruments all over the world.

"All of these projects," London says, "have helped me to express, reconnect with, deepen, and expand my Jewish identity in one way or another."

Yet London, like the other artists in this chapter, has been able to move beyond narrow self-expression and has attempted to reach out to others through his work. Just as some of the treasures of Jewish culture were revealed to him many years ago, London sees it as part of his task as a musician and a Jew to expose other disconnected Jews to the hidden joys of their heritage: "Being a musician working in the field of Jew-ish music has meant that I am always engaged in a dialectic about Jewish issues—political, religious, cultural, aesthetic, mystical, and practical. My research and work has given me a much richer vocabulary and broader palette of songs, ideas, ways of celebrating and observing. Most important, and in the most elemental way, my music keeps me in contact with other Jews."

Jewish culture, liturgy, and ritual have *opened* doors for London, not closed them. They have been a fount of creativity and a path to community.

But London has had his share of frustrations with institu-tional Judaism as well. "The artist's relationship to organized religion has always been problematic," he concedes. "Often there is absolutely no acknowledgment of the benefit of the arts to Jewish life and community. Even when the benefit is seen, the Jewish organization may have its own agenda or be unwilling to take the kinds of risks that an artist may want to take. Sometimes things have worked out. The National Foun-dation for Jewish Culture commissioned me to compose *Dav-enen* ("Praying" in Yiddish) for the experimental Pilobolus Dance Theater, and through the Klezmatics I've worked on *Freedom Songs* for the Museum of Jewish Heritage and a proj-ect called 'Woody Guthrie's Happy Joyous Chanukah,' thanks to Woody's daughter Nora and his archives—eight new Chanukah songs, one for each night, with music set to never-before-recorded lyrics by Guthrie about his experiences with Jewish life and culture on Coney Island."

Taking risks and embracing uncertainty—and boldly, often provocatively, celebrating both—will always play an impor-tant role in London's art. His identity as a Jew and his cre-ations as a musician have become beautifully entwined, like the braided candle that is used for the *Havdalah* ceremony that ends the Jewish Sabbath at sunset: "My work will keep me constantly engaged in all things Jewish. My family and I are engaged in an ongoing dialogue with Judaism—the religion, the traditions, the people, the culture. We are on a path, and we don't know where it will lead."

It has long been observed that various forms of artistic expression—from Greek tragedies to Norse epic poetry—trace their origins to religious ideas and rituals. The rites these later performances emerged from often involved music, song, mythic narrative, drama, and other creative elements. But this same phenomenon can happen in reverse, and we're witnessing it right now. The arts can, and in many cases have, become a gateway back to the world of organized religion.

Contemporary artists, sometimes intentionally and sometimes not, frequently form a kind of bridge between their work and religious life. It may not be religion as we ordinarily think of that word and institution—it may not include a lot of ritual observance, or formal worship, or direct talk about the divine. Yet art, through its wide range of manifestations and expressions, can pry open our minds, hearts, and souls in ways that few other activities are capable of doing.

Those creative expressions may at times be unconventional, even unsettling, but they can also be revelatory—and revelation is at the very foundation of religious life. Are we open and receptive to *that* message? Can we shake loose our baggage, our negative associations with religion? The arts may inspire us. They may disclose new, enthralling ways of thinking, seeing, and feeling. But religion takes all that a step further.

It also takes us beyond ourselves.

Sure, we can say that we reject Judaism. We can get all worked up and rebel against it until we're blue in the face. But when push comes to shove, more often than not—if we're thoughtful and self-aware—we'll eventually recognize that our struggle is *itself* an engagement, a relationship, a deep and profound connection that transcends any surface conflict or obstacle we might confront.

That's gonzo personified.

So attend a local Jewish arts festival. Go to a Jewish concert, play, or film series. If you're an artist yourself, keep at it, but explore some fresh themes, maybe ones that make you uncomfortable (like your religious identity). Find a bridge. Expand your conception of what it means for something, or someone, to be Jewish. Then see if your rebellion isn't just a mask for a desire to return.

"Shock and awe" might be a country's military doctrine for waging war, but it is also an effective way of using new tactics to break through our many defenses and open us up to a world of faith and fellowship.

CONCLUSION

IF JUDAISM IS TO BE RELEVANT and meaningful to this generation of Jews, it must recapture the prophetic spirit, the gonzo impulse that has animated our people for so many centuries and has led to so much creativity and achievement. When we look around us, we see that the world is—as it has always been—wounded. We see hatred and violence, hunger and poverty, hypocrisy and corruption, polluted waters and global warming. It is our sacred task as Jews to *rail* against this condition, to strive with all our might to fight the status quo and to mend our unjust society and injured planet.

That is the age-old principle of *tikkun olam,* of fixing our fractured world.

In one of his books Albert Camus asks himself, "What is a rebel?" His answer reveals the paradox of the prophet and the ambiguity of our own struggle: "A man who says no, but whose refusal does not imply a renunciation. He is also a man who says yes, from the moment he makes his first gesture of rebellion."

And what is the rebel saying "yes" to? Why is rebellion an act of affirmation rather than one of renunciation? Because when we reject a broken status quo we are, in essence, embracing a vision of a better state, an improved situation. We can fight against a particular foreign policy without rejecting our governmental system as a whole—and we can fight against poor expressions of the Jewish religion without renouncing Judaism itself. The rebel's soul isn't rooted in negativity. The rebel fights *for* something in the same breath that he or she fights *against* something else.

Ours is a battle for a robust, revitalized Judaism. Passion, not rage, ought to be the emotion that inspires us and the motivation for our actions.

It's not enough to be angry with the powers that be. Who wants to just spit into the wind? It's the moral and religious obligation of every one of us to (sometimes loudly and unabashedly) call truth to power, but we must also offer an alternative, a constructive solution to the problems of contemporary Jewish life. That's what I've attempted to do with this book, based on my own experiences and observations.

It won't be easy. We'll have to rethink our institutions and practices. We'll need to create new ones. And we'll have to change our own mind-set.

But it's starting to happen. We're seeing more clearly than ever what today's Jews really crave, and are beginning to demand: a religion that helps us to feel, and to feel deeply; that is inviting, accessible, and accepting; that stimulates our senses and our souls; that encourages participation, not passivity; that comforts us when we're in pain and pushes us when we're lazy; that gives us community, but also opportunities for self-expression; that is transporting, positive, and at times even fun.

This might seem like a pretty tall order, but God's no short-order cook. Our nourishment is there—all we need to do is sit down at the table.

As a gonzo journalist, Hunter S. Thompson revolutionized his field and inserted himself into the center of the story, and he did it with a brashness that did not always sit well with his publishers. Jews today need to act—and act *out*—with that same raucous bravado, to place ourselves squarely in the center of the story and the action, even if it is disquieting to the leaders of a complacent Jewish establishment.

We need to reclaim our rebel roots.

Gonzo Judaism is about trying to recover and reaffirm that revolutionary impulse and using it to reshape the Judaism we've inherited from the previous generation, a Judaism that many of us find out of touch, banal, irrelevant, ossified, and boring. It's about taking risks and thinking freely and expansively, yet it's also about looking back into the riches of our past in order to move forward into our future.

It's a return as well as a rejection, an excavation as much as a demolition.

Gonzo Judaism embraces this paradox—and accepting paradox is what postmodern Jews, and their Judaism, need more than anything else.

Does that make this approach radical or conservative? I couldn't care less. It's probably a little of both. What really matters is that it provides an answer, a way out of the wilderness. Or maybe it provides a way of viewing the wilderness *itself* as the solution—not as a place of danger, but as a place of protection, a sanctuary for souls lost in the intellectual, societal, and geopolitical conflicts of modernity.

Our first step must be an internal one—we must look within before we can march ahead. We need to get over ourselves and over our childhood baggage. We need to move beyond the self, beyond negative associations and stereotypes, and reach out to others. Only then will we truly be liberated. Only then will the power of ethical *and* ritual behavior sink in and lead us down the path of a purpose-driven life.

Religion, at its best, can be the greatest of adventures, a

rocket ride for the mind, spirit, and even body. It can be countercultural and cool. But a gonzo model of our religion isn't something that can be forced. If we try too hard to be hip in our attempts to draw disaffected Jews back to Judaism, we won't just look desperate—we'll become disingenuous posers. And brutal honesty is what gonzo is all about.

The Jewish community has to expand itself—not quantitatively, but qualitatively. Like a very large tent, we must offer people multiple entry points. The synagogue, while important, is just one of them. For some of us, nature will be the gateway to our spiritual tradition; for others, it will be the arts and culture; for still others, it will be a sense of elemental belonging that only a new kind of tribalism can provide.

As is the case in so many other areas of life, much of the most vibrant, cutting-edge, and exciting activity is happening at the margins.

The fringe is Judaism's foundry.

To hell with continuity. We are in a period of transition, and it is *dis*continuity that will carry us, as it always has, into the next stage of Jewish life. What exactly will our fresh, refashioned forms of Jewish expression—and, as long as we're asking, the larger expressions of organized religion in general—look like? The only thing that we can know for sure is that we can't know anything for sure.

With one exception: We have to jump into the fray if we want to be active players, rather than mere bystanders, in this historic transformation.

Franz Kafka thought that writing could serve as an ax that would break "the frozen sea inside us." I believe with all of my being that religion, when done right, can achieve the same objective—and then some.

Gonzo Judaism, through its boldness, potency, and exuberant spirit, can shatter our fortifications and inspire us to open our hearts and tents.

It can light our way in an era of darkness.

It can give us direction in an age of confusion.

And it can suffuse our hungry souls with hope.

WHERE A GONZO JEW CAN GO

IF YOU AGREED with even a few of the ideas behind a gonzo approach to Jewish life, don't just sit on your butt and criticize our entrenched institutions and leaders for being so crappy. Before you even put down this book, go do something. Join the fight: rebel, revitalize, reshape your religious tradition. If you won't, who will? That's a huge part of what it *means* to be a gonzo Jew—to take action. There's a world of possibilities waiting for you to explore.

What follows is a representative selection of organizations, synagogues, and grassroots groups and networks that—in my view and that of many rabbinic colleagues and other Jewish professionals—offer dynamic programs and new ways of thinking about contemporary Judaism. Some of the names will be familiar, as they were cited in this book; others will be new, though they may in fact have been on the Jewish scene for many years.

Check out the Web sites and see what you think. There are groups devoted to community service and social justice, both here and in the third world; immersion experiences and spiritual growth; outreach to interfaith couples and families; activism and advocacy in Israel; creating Jewish programs grounded in the arts or in the environment; developing online communities of learning, dialogue, and debate.

If it's a full-fledged synagogue you're looking for, I've high-lighted some congregations (by region and city) that I believe are among the most vigorous and forward-thinking around. Some of them have been in existence for only a few years; others have been active for decades. In some cases, it is in the larger, old-school synagogues where, ironically, much of the bolder and more dynamic programming is taking place—depending on the vision of their leadership and how willing they are to reinvent themselves and to rethink their missions. The shuls that I've selected span the major Jewish movements: Reform, Conservative, Reconstructionist, Orthodox, and also independent. When possible I've tried to achieve a denominational balance within the various cities, but my guideline for inclusion on the list was innovation and vitality, not ideological affiliation.

So give one a shot. Don't separate yourself from the community. *Help* it. It needs your involvement and input as much as you need it—even if, at this particular moment in your life, you don't think you do.

People change. Religions change. But the latter doesn't change without the participation, and sometimes pressure, of the former.

ORGANIZATIONS AND INSTITUTIONS

AJWS: American Jewish World Service
www.ajws.org

AVODAH: The Jewish Service Corps
www.avodah.net

Beit Midrash: A Liberal Yeshivah in Jerusalem
www.huc.edu/liberalyeshivah

Birthright Israel
www.birthrightisrael.com

The Brandeis-Bardin Institute
www.thebbi.org

Chochmat HaLev Meditation Center
www.chochmat.org

CLAL: The National Jewish Center for Learning and Leadership
www.clal.org

COEJL: The Coalition on the Environment and Jewish Life
www.coejl.org

Combined Jewish Philanthropies
www.cjp.org

Dell Jewish Community Campus
www.shalomaustin.org

The Educational Alliance
www.edalliance.org

Elat Chayyim Center for Jewish Spirituality
www.isabellafreedman.org

Hebrew College
www.hebrewcollege.edu

Hillel: The Foundation for Jewish Campus Life
www.hillel.org

Institute for Jewish Spirituality
www.ijs-online.org

The Institute for Southern Jewish Life
www.isjl.org

Isabella Freedman Jewish Retreat Center
www.isabellafreedman.org

JCC Association
www.jcca.org

Jewish Community Project
www.jcpdowntown.org

Jewish Community Relations Council of Greater Boston
www.jcrcboston.org

Jewish Education Service of North America
www.jesna.org

Jewish Outreach Institute
www.joi.org

Kolot: Center for Jewish Women's and Gender Studies
www.kolot.org

Ma'yan: The Jewish Women's Project
www.mayan.org

MAZON: A Jewish Response to Hunger
www.mazon.org

Metivta: A Center for Contemplative Judaism
www.metivta.org

National Foundation for Jewish Culture
www.jewishculture.org

New Israel Fund: Promoting Equality and Social Justice for All
Israelis
www.nif.org

New York Kollel
www.huc.edu/kollel

OTZMA: The Ultimate Real Life Experience
www.otzma.org

PANIM: The Institute for Jewish Leadership and Values
www.panim.org

PEJE: The Partnership for Excellence in Jewish Education
www.peje.org

Ramah Darom: The Center for Southern Jewry
www.ramahdarom.org

Religious Action Center of Reform Judaism
www.rac.org.

The Shalom Center
www.shalomctr.org

STAR [Synagogues: Transformation and Renewal]
www.starsynagogue.org

The Steinhardt Foundation for Jewish Life
www.jewishlife.org

UJA–Federation of New York
www.ujafedny.org

Union for Reform Judaism Kallah
www.urj.org/educate/kallah

The 92nd Street Y
www.92y.org

92YTribeca
www.92ytribeca.org

SYNAGOGUES

Northeast

Adas Israel Congregation (Washington, DC)
www.adasisrael.org

Adat Shalom Reconstructionist Congregation (Bethesda, MD)
www.adatshalom.net

The Bolton Street Synagogue (Baltimore, MD)
www.boltonstreet.org

Central Synagogue (New York, NY)
www.centralsynagogue.org

Congregation Ansche Chesed (New York, NY)
www.anschechesed.org

Congregation B'nai Jeshurun (New York, NY)
www.bj.org

Congregation Dor Hadash (Pittsburgh, PA)
www.jrf.org/dorhadash

Congregation Dorshei Tzedek (West Newton, MA)
www.dorsheitzedek.org

Congregation Emanu-El (New York, NY)
www.emanuelnyc.org

Congregation Kehillath Israel (Brookline, MA)
www.congki.org

Congregation Kol Ami (White Plains, NY)
www.nykolami.org

Congregation Shaarei Tefillah (Newton Center, MA)
www.shaarei.org

Germantown Jewish Centre (Philadelphia, PA)
www.germantownjewishcentre.org

Hebrew Institute of Riverdale (Riverdale, NY)
www.hir.org

Kehilat Hadar (New York, NY)
www.kehilathadar.org

Mishkan Shalom (Philadelphia, PA)
www.mishkan.org

The New Shul (New York, NY)
www.newshul.org

Reform Congregation Keneseth Israel (Elkins Park, PA)
www.kenesethisrael.org

Rodef Shalom Congregation (Pittsburgh, PA)
www.rodefshalom.org

Society for the Advancement of Judaism (New York, NY)
www.thesaj.org

Temple Beth Elohim (Wellesley, MA)
www.bethelohim-wellesley.org

Temple Israel/The Riverway Project (Boston, MA)
www.riverwayproject.org
www.tisrael.org

Temple Micah (Washington, DC)
www.templemicah.org

Town and Village Synagogue (New York, NY)
www.tandv.org

Midwest

Adat Shalom Synagogue (Farmington Hills, MI)
www.adatshalom.org

Anshe Chesed Fairmount Temple (Beachwood, OH)
www.fairmounttemple.org

Anshe Emet Synagogue (Chicago, IL)
www.ansheemet.org

Anshe Sholom B'nai Israel Congregation (Chicago, IL)
www.asbi.org

Bais Abraham Congregation (St. Louis, MO)
www.baisabe.com

Beth Emet the Free Synagogue (Evanston, IL)
www.bethemet.org

Beth Jacob Congregation (Mendota Heights, MN)
www.beth-jacob.org

Central Reform Congregation (St. Louis, MO)
www.centralreform.org

Congregation Sukkat Shalom (Wilmette, IL)
www.sukkatshalom.org

Kol HaLev (University Heights, OH)
www.kolhalev.net

The Park Synagogue (Cleveland Heights, OH)
www.parksyn.org

Shir Hadash (Northbrook, IL)
www.shir-hadash.org

Shir Tikvah (Minneapolis, MN)
www.shirtikvah.net

Temple Beth Emeth (Ann Arbor, MI)
www.templebethemeth.org

Temple Israel (West Bloomfield, MI)
www.temple-israel.org

Temple Sholom (Chicago, IL)
www.sholomchicago.org

South

Congregation Albert (Albuquerque, NM)
www.congregationalbert.org

Congregation Beth Torah (Richardson, TX)
www.congregationbethtorah.org

Congregation Beth Yeshurun (Houston, TX)
www.bethyeshurun.org

Congregation Emanu El (Houston, TX)
www.emanuelhouston.org

Congregation Or Hadash (Atlanta, GA)
www.or-hadash.org

Congregation Shearith Israel (Atlanta, GA)
www.shearithisrael.com

Congregation Shearith Israel (Dallas, TX)
www.shearith.org

Ramat Shalom (Plantation, FL)
www.ramatshalom.org

The Temple (Atlanta, GA)
www.the-temple.org

Temple Beth El (Boca Raton, FL)
www.tbeboca.com

Temple Beth El (Charlotte, NC)
www.beth-el.com

Temple Beth Shalom (Austin, TX)
www.bethshalomaustin.org

Temple Chai (Phoenix, AZ)
www.templechai.com

Temple Emanu-El (Dallas, TX)
www.tedallas.org

Temple Israel (Longwood, FL)
www.tiflorida.org

Temple Israel (Miami, FL)
www.templeisrael.net

West

B'nai David–Judea Congregation (Los Angeles, CA)
www.bnaidavid.com

Congregation Beth Am (Los Altos Hills, CA)
www.betham.org

Congregation Beth Am (San Diego, CA)
www.betham.com

Congregation Beth David (Saratoga, CA)
www.beth-david.org

Congregation Beth Israel (Berkeley, CA)
www.beth-israel.berkeley.ca.us

Congregation Beth Israel (Portland, OR)
www.bethisrael-pdx.org

Congregation Beth Sholom (San Francisco, CA)
www.bethsholomsf.org

The Congregation Emanu-El (San Francisco, CA)
www.emanuelsf.org

Congregation Emanuel (Denver, CO)
www.congregationemanuel.com

Congregation Har HaShem (Boulder, CO)
www.harhashem.org

Congregation Kol Ami (West Hollywood, CA)
www.kol-ami.org

Congregation Kol HaNeshamah (Seattle, WA)
www.kol-haneshamah.org

Congregation Kol Shofar (Tiburon, CA)
www.kolshofar.org

Congregation Ohr HaTorah (Los Angeles, CA)
www.ohrhatorah.org

Havurah Shalom (Portland, OR)
www.havurahshalom.org

The Hebrew Educational Alliance (Denver, CO)
www.headenver.org

Herzl-Ner Tamid Conservative Congregation (Mercer Island, WA)
www.herzl-ner-tamid.org

IKAR (Los Angeles, CA)
www.ikar-la.org

Sinai Temple (Los Angeles, CA)
www.sinaitemple.org

Stephen S. Wise Temple (Los Angeles, CA)
www.sswt.org

Temple Beth Am/The Library Minyan (Los Angeles, CA)
www.tbala.org

Temple Solel (Cardiff-by-the-Sea, CA)
www.templesolel.net

University Synagogue (Irvine, CA)
www.universitysynagogue.org

GRASSROOTS GROUPS AND NETWORKS

Adventure Rabbi
www.adventurerabbi.com

Avoda Arts: Innovative Education Through the Arts
www.avodaarts.org

Burning Bush Adventures
www.sover.net/~bethelvt/bba.html

Generation J
www.generationj.com

GesherCity: Bridging Young Adults to the Jewish Community
www.geshercity.org

Hazon: New Vision, Inclusive Community, Outdoor and
Environmental Education
www.hazon.org

JDub Records
www.jdubrecords.org

Jew School: Alternative Views and Culture
www.jewschool.com

Jewish Adventure Travel
www.newshul.org

Jewish Coalition for Service
www.jewishservice.org

Jewish Community Action: Organizing for Justice
www.jewishcommunityaction.org

Jewish Council on Urban Affairs
www.jcua.org

Jewish Organizing Initiative
www.jewishorganizing.org

Jews United for Justice
www.jufj.org

JewZ
www.jewz.com

JInsider: Jewish Intelligence
www.jinsider.com

Kosher Expeditions
www.kosherexpeditions.com

Koshertreks
www.koshertreks.com

Limmud NY: Jewish Learning Without Limits
www.limmudny.org

MATAN: The Gift of Jewish Learning for Every Child
www.matankids.org

Mosaic Outdoor Clubs of America
www.mosaicoutdoor.org

My Jewish Learning: The Personal Gateway to Jewish Exploration
www.myjewishlearning.com

National Havurah Committee
www.havurah.org

Progressive Jewish Alliance   .
www.pjalliance.org

Reboot: A Network for Jewish Innovation
www.rebooters.net

Ritual Well: Ceremonies for Jewish Living
www.ritualwell.org

Storahtelling: Jewish Ritual Theater Revived
www.storahtelling.org

Teva Adventure
www.tevaadventure.org

TorahTrek: Spiritual Wilderness Adventures
www.torahtrek.com

Travel Jewish
www.traveljewish.com

Yachad: Jewish Housing and Community Development
www.yachad-dc.org

WHAT A GONZO JEW CAN READ

Two MILLENNIA BEFORE OUR TIME, the biblical figure
Kohelet lamented over the fact that even then there was no
possible way a human being could read everything that he or
she wanted to, and that study was an endless, exhausting process: "Of making many books there is no end, and much study
is a weariness of the flesh" (Ecclesiastes 12:12). Yes, the books
keep flying off the presses. No, we'll never get close to reading
all the ones we want to. And, yes, it can sometimes seem like
the entire enterprise of acquiring information and knowledge
is an exercise in futility.

Yet Kohelet is countered elsewhere in the Jewish tradition,
where we're taught, "It is not up to you to complete the task,
but neither are you free to desist from it" (*Pirke Avot*). Don't get
so intimidated that you're too scared to start—just suck it up
and get going. Despair is for the weak and fearful, not the gonzo
Jew. You don't have to finish, to pretend you've mastered thousands of years of accumulated Jewish wisdom. You just need
to grab a book and begin.

The previous section listed ways of connecting with others
on your journey into Judaism and Jewish community. But if
you're not yet ready for that, or if you have nowhere to go in
your area, or if you just want to be by yourself, the following
list of (highly subjective) recommended books might be the

answer—at a minimum, it will keep you busy for a while. Some of the books deal with Jewish thought, history, and culture; some relate to the Bible, the holidays, and religious practice; some examine Jewish mysticism and spirituality; and some aren't even overtly Jewish, but are nevertheless written in the *spirit* of a gonzo way of seeing and living in the world.

Although this list is meant only as a stepping-stone to further and deeper exploration, it will provide you with building blocks as you begin to lay the groundwork of your own Jewish identity in this new, perplexing century.

Books

Alter, Robert. 1983. *The Art of Biblical Narrative.* New York: Perseus Publishing.

———. 1987. *The Art of Biblical Poetry.* New York: Perseus Publishing.

Becker, Ernest. 1997. *The Denial of Death.* New York: Free Press.

Blumenthal, David R. 1994. *God at the Center.* Northvale, NJ: Jason Aronson, Inc.

Borowitz, Eugene B. 1983. *Choices in Modern Jewish Thought.* West Orange, NJ: Behrman House.

Buber, Martin. 1996. *I and Thou.* New York: Touchstone.

———. 1991. *Tales of the Hasidim.* New York: Schocken Books.

Buxbaum, Yitzhak. 1994. *Jewish Spiritual Practices.* Northvale, NJ: Jason Aronson, Inc.

Camus, Albert. 1992. *The Rebel.* New York: Random House.

Carmi, T. 1981. *The Penguin Book of Hebrew Verse.* New York: Penguin Books.

Cohen, Arthur A., and Paul Mendes-Flohr. 1986. *Contemporary Jewish Religious Thought.* New York: Macmillan.

Cuddihy, John Murray. 1987. *The Ordeal of Civility.* Boston: Beacon Press.

Fishbane, Michael. 1996. *The Kiss of God.* Seattle: University of Washington Press.

Fromm, Erich. 1991. *You Shall Be As Gods.* New York: Random House.

Gillman, Neil. 2004. *The Death of Death.* Woodstock, VT: Jewish Lights Publishing.

Goldberg, J. J. 1997. *Jewish Power.* New York: Perseus Books.

Green, Arthur. 1988. *Jewish Spirituality I.* New York: Crossroad Publishing.

———. 1989. *Jewish Spirituality II.* New York: Crossroad Publishing.

———. 1992. *Tormented Master.* Woodstock, VT: Jewish Lights Publishing.

———, and Barry W. Holtz. 1993. *Your Word Is Fire.* Woodstock, VT: Jewish Lights Publishing.

Greenberg, Irving. 1988. *The Jewish Way.* New York: Touchstone.

Harrison, Robert Pogue. 1992. *Forests.* Chicago: University of Chicago Press.

Hertzberg, Arthur. 1997. *The Zionist Idea.* Philadelphia: Jewish Publication Society.

Heschel, Abraham Joshua. 1995. *A Passion for Truth.* Woodstock, VT: Jewish Lights Publishing.

———. 1988. *The Sabbath.* New York: Farrar, Straus and Giroux.

Holtz, Barry W. 1984. *Back to the Sources.* New York: Touchstone.

Joselit, Jenna Weissman. 1994. *The Wonders of America.* New York: Henry Holt and Company.

Jung, C. G. 1960. *Psychology and Religion.* New Haven: Yale University Press.

Kaplan, Aryeh. 1985. *Jewish Meditation.* New York: Schocken Books.

Kierkegaard, Søren. 1986. *Fear and Trembling.* New York: Penguin Books.

Lasch, Christopher. 1991. *The Culture of Narcissism.* New York: Norton.

Matt, Daniel C. 1996. *The Essential Kabbalah.* New York: HarperCollins.

Mendes-Flohr, Paul, and Jehuda Reinharz. 1995. *The Jew in the Modern World.* New York: Oxford University Press.

Neusner, Jacob. 1991. *The Enchantments of Judaism.* Tampa, FL: University of South Florida Press.

Nietzsche, Friedrich. 1989. *Beyond Good and Evil.* New York: Random House.

————. 1989. *Thus Spoke Zarathustra.* New York: Random House.

Plaskow, Judith. 1990. *Standing Again at Sinai.* New York: HarperCollins.

Pogrebin, Letty Cottin. 1992. *Deborah, Golda, and Me.* New York: Anchor Books.

Rosenzweig, Franz. 1985. *The Star of Redemption.* Notre Dame: University of Notre Dame Press.

Sachar, Howard M. 2003. *A History of Israel.* New York: Random House.

Sarna, Jonathan. 2004. *American Judaism.* New Haven: Yale University Press.

Scholem, Gershom. 1995. *Major Trends in Jewish Mysticism.* New York: Schocken Books.

Schwarz, Sidney. 2000. *Finding a Spiritual Home.* New York: Jossey-Bass.

Shanks, Hershel. 1999. *Ancient Israel.* Englewood Cliffs, NJ: Prentice Hall.

Soloveitchik, Joseph B. 1996. *The Lonely Man of Faith.* Northvale, NJ: Jason Aronson, Inc.

Spiegelman, Art. 1986. *Maus I.* New York: Random House.

————. 1991. *Maus II.* New York: Random House.

Storr, Anthony. 1989. *Solitude.* New York: Ballantine Books.

Strassfeld, Michael. 2001. *The Jewish Holidays.* New York: HarperCollins.

Telushkin, Joseph. 1997. *Jewish Literacy.* New York: William Morrow and Company.

Thompson, Hunter S. 1998. *Fear and Loathing in Las Vegas.* New York: Vintage Books.

————. 1995. *Hell's Angels.* New York: Ballantine Books.

Vermes, G. 2004. *The Complete Dead Sea Scrolls in English.* New York: Penguin Books.

Waskow, Arthur. 1991. *Seasons of Our Joy.* Boston: Beacon Press.

Magazines/Periodicals

The Blueprint	*Lilith*
Contact	*Moment*
The Forward	*Sh'ma*
Heeb	*The Tablet*
The Jerusalem Report	*Tikkun*
The Jewish Week	*Zeek*

ACKNOWLEDGMENTS

THIS WAS A BOOK I DIDN'T WANT TO WRITE.

I'm a rabbi, I thought. *My whole life revolves around Jews. I teach them. I counsel them. I lead services for them. I officiate at their life-cycle events. They're my colleagues. Why the hell would I want to do anything more with or for these wacky, stubborn, opinionated people, like writing a book?*

But writing this book has been a blast, and I owe that to my agent, Linda Loewenthal, for reining me in from the wider, generic world of spirituality and forcing me to look deep within my own community and faith.

I've loathed some of what I've witnessed. I've also loved some of it. That's what this book has ultimately been about. Thanks, Linda, for urging me to put into print what I've been thinking and speaking about for more than fifteen years—and for encouraging me to do so without holding (almost) anything back.

I am especially grateful to my congregation and spiritual home, The New Shul, for a decade of mutual support and respect. As I transition into the next chapter of my career, I will treasure my new status as Rabbi Emeritus.

Thank you to all those synagogues, organizations, and other groups around the country for inviting me into your communities to lecture and learn. Much that is between this book's covers is a direct outgrowth of my experiences with you.

There are too many wonderful teachers to whom I am indebted to list here, so I won't. But I want to acknowledge two mentors in particular whom I've never even met personally, John Cuddihy and Jonathan Sarna, for opening my eyes through their own writings and insights into Jewish life, history, culture, and religion.

Each in his or her own way—Rabbi Andrew Bachman, Matthew Baigell, Rabbi Daniel Bronstein, Rabbi Hayim Herring, Gabrielle Lipson, Tonda Marton, Aliza Mazor, Andrea Most, Jackie Payson, Rabbi Sid Schwarz, Don Sylvan, Laurie Wessely, and Jon Woocher—has offered invaluable assistance and support, as have all those who were gracious enough to have shared their personal experiences and journeys with me.

I want to express my heartfelt appreciation to the directors and associate directors of the regional offices of the Union for Reform Judaism, the United Synagogue of Conservative Judaism, and the Jewish Reconstructionist Federation for their thoughtful guidance, generosity of time and spirit, and commitment to pluralism in helping me with my survey of synagogues. There's some very good, innovative stuff taking place today, and I wouldn't have known about a lot of it without their aid. Through my frank, honest discussions with them I feel far more optimistic about Jewish congregational life in North America than I did when I began the book.

The publisher of this paperback edition, Trumpeter, deserves special gratitude. This is our second book together, and it has been a true pleasure working with such a wonderful, dedicated team. I thank Peter Turner, president; Beth Frankl, my amazing editor and friend; and Julie Saidenberg and Jennifer Campaniolo for their continued belief in and advocacy for my work.

ABOUT THE AUTHOR

NILES ELLIOT GOLDSTEIN is the founder and Rabbi Emeritus of The New Shul, an innovative and independent congregation in Greenwich Village, New York. He lectures widely on religion and spirituality and has taught at New York University and the Hebrew Union College–Jewish Institute of Religion. Goldstein is the National Jewish Chaplain for the Federal Law Enforcement Officers Association, a member of PEN and the Renaissance Institute, and was the voice behind "Ask the Rabbi" on the Microsoft Network. His essays, op-ed pieces, and poetry have appeared in *Newsweek,* the *Los Angeles Times, Newsday,* and many other publications, and he is the award-winning author or editor of nine books. Goldstein has been featured in *Time,* the *New York Times,* the *Wall Street Journal,* the *Christian Science Monitor,* the *New York Observer, New York Magazine, Real Simple,* and *Glamour* as well as on national and international television and radio such as *Dateline*, CNN, MSNBC, NPR, Voice of America, and the BBC. He lives in Brooklyn, New York.